POETRAITS

BY
ROSÉ

sp
SYNERGETIC PRESS
Santa Fe, New Mexico

First edition.
Published by Synergetic Press
7 Silver Hills Road
Santa Fe, NM 87505 USA

www.synergeticpress.com

Cover design by Elemental Graphics.
Cover Art: Facefield; 2000, digital painting by permission of
James G. Wrinkle

ISBN 0 907791 34 4

To
Sweet Linda
of my heart

POETRAITS

Poetraits is not a Southern drawl
But images in words
Pictures of people I recall
Creatures who on this planet crawl
Whose spirits soar with the birds.

I've painted some pictures of people
On paper in poems not paints
Their quirks and their noses
Their postures and poses
If you're one of them
Please, no complaints.

Contents

WONDERFUL WOMEN

When they are young and beautiful
Still turning somersaults
And sleek and smooth and plump as porpoise
We watch them growing old and beautiful
Defying time's assaults
Absorbed in their metamorphosis.

When they are young and beautiful
Completely without faults
We revel in their strength of purpose
When they are old and beautiful
House them in underwater vaults
And kiss them whenever they surface.

FELICIA

The cottonwoods their limbs all stretching
Like elephants their trunks just touching
Form canopies their branches yawning
Above the golden dawn.
Returning to their beds aglowing
Flowers pretend they're just growing
When it's quite clear that they've been throwing
A party on the lawn.

About the grounds mists caracoling
Like pools of waves their curls unrolling
While arm in arm the ghosts are strolling
Along the avenues
Where herds of cottonwoods are filling
Root trunks, their leaves like fountains spilling
It's morning at Felicia's — thrilling
Far better than a cruise.

BARBARA

I hear you're going on a cruise
To gorgeous island rendezvous
To stroll those rolling avenues
And loll on sunny decks
To climb up dizzy mountain trails
Where drifts of snow explode like sails
And clouds below float by like whales
And people look like specks.

I know you've read the travel books
And picked out all the perfect nooks
Selected several gourmet cooks
To always be at hand.
Make sure to pack your evening clothes
Robes, gowns, smart shoes, fancy chapeaux
They dress for dinner, I suppose
Or so I understand.

Yes, understanding is the key
That opens up Life's mystery
That strings together you and me
And all the other souls —
Who wait in line right from their birth
For tickets, a king's ransom worth
On the next cruise ship leaving Earth
The Gods at the controls.

LINDA

To show my love for you I'll slave
My life away inside a cave
My rights to everything I'll waive
To show my love for you

Against all odds for you I'll fight
Defend your honor day and night
I'll push, I'll scream, I'll kick, I'll bite
To show my love for you

To show my love I'll wear what's torn
Unkempt, I'll go about forlorn
Stand on my head until it's worn
Away with love for you

I'll fast until I die of thirst
I'll volunteer to be the first
To hold my breath until I burst
To show my love for you

To show my love, dear, I'll keep hopping
Yes, starting now and never stopping
But I will not go Christmas shopping
To show my love for you.

FRAN

I found your card deep in my wallet
Jay Landesman PRODUCE of qualit
Y, I'm sure, but now's no time for frivolit
Y – I'm placing an order:

Please send Xpress fast as you can
Eighteen nice melons from Iran
Those luscious ones of coral streaked with tan
We gorged on at the border

I also need a bushel each
Of gold sapote and of peach
Those that into my hands themselves do reach
To cure a slight disorder

I hear your wife's in produce too
Preparing fruits of speckled hue
Ripe poems as sweet as Persian honeydew
I'd like to reward her

With an image I remember
Poetry at Sev's, December
Fran, caught in the fire's dying ember
And you leaning toward her.

NORMA

Norma, across the states we go
From New York to New Mexico
Been five and twenty years or so
But seems like yesterday

There's a hill that we ascended
Before the Eastern mountains ended
Where Jimmy tilted half suspended
I saw him float away

And Colorado dawned supreme
House on a bridge over a stream
Saw Libre born out of a dream
Under the Milky Way

We pushed on to the Rio Grande
Where the gorge drops a mile and splits the land
We rested — then on through the sun and the sand
On the trail to Santa Fe

Where I saw you last week at a dinner
Looking just like an angelic sinner
Quite aglow with a light that is inner
And beams through your mortal clay.

BELLA

The telephone's not such a bad device
Although I really hate to hear it ring
And thru my blissful meditations slice
As shrill as a bird with a broken wing
Don't pick it up unless you want advice
Or gossip, slander, bad news, quarreling
Or care to learn about a relative's afflictions
It's hard to live without this worst of all addictions.

The comfortable clasp of the receiver
That clings so lovingly to lip and ear
A caller never wants that touch to leave her
Nor the voice within the wire to disappear
Talk on thru meals, thru sleep, thru sex and fever
Despite hoarse throat, each day of every year
The telephone's not such a bad device, I swear
I talked with Bella yesterday and walk on air.

GAIL

I read that poem again the other day.
Many a time in the past forty years
Those words have leaped the page into my eyes
And always my thoughts travel the same way
I break into a smile and shed some tears
And maybe laugh a bit between the sighs
Remembering how you dreamed it would be
Three old white heads you and Barry and me

On a stretch of sand on a beach somewhere
The sun on our hands the salt on our skin
Watching the waves as they beat on the shore
And one of us sits in an old beach chair
And all of us watch as the waves come in
On a beach somewhere in the ocean's roar
Content, mellowed by all kinds of weather
Alone, just the three of us together.

And this last reading now of Adam's Curse
Sent such a pang throughout my every nerve
To think that there is naught we can reverse
And naught but memories we can preserve
How a so indifferent universe
Will run right over us rather than swerve
Will leave us broken in its aftermath
To rise amazed and find ourselves still on the path.

BETTY

I'm always thinking about you
'Cause you are my shining star
Your memory paints a tattoo
That I wear on my face like a scar

And just like those ancient Romans
Who peeled back their togas to show
Wounds proudly worn like bright omens
O so many campaigns ago

And just like those Prussian swordsmen
Who dueling would offer the face
Who counted their scars as awards men
Of honor display like old lace

I also wear proudly upon it
On my face after so many years
A scar like a ruined sonnet
Singing your song in my ears
A mark like a royal sonnet
Singing your song in my ears.

NICTE–HA

Now is that magic day that comes but once
A year when we've almost forgotten
That time can fly so fast, that life confronts
Us all, the blessed and the misbegotten
The rogue, the rosy rascal, sage and dunce
The fine and noble ones, the base and rotten
It's here before we know it's come again
And so I'm picking up my fountain pen

To wish you all the very best of luck
On a quarter century's completion
Without you running totally amuck
Like Shakespeare's jealous tormented Venetian
My lovely daughter I am wonderstruck
That you, like morning dew, God's secretion
Can wash my cares away with just the thought
Of the wonder that Lin and I have wrought.

BELLA

You can have other lads, my lass
Have lovers, husbands, men
The whole world will before you pass
And you may take your choice — alas
Of Fathers there's but one.

FELICIA

Ignore the tales she tells you
How she was far away
In some other country
On that fateful day

Forget the pretty stories
She'll weave to cover up
How she was at a supper club
Just sitting down to sup

O it was just impossible
She'd never be caught dead
In such a place, she'd rather lose
Her poise, her maidenhead

There was no way in all the world
She'd rather lose her yacht
Why, just to think that she'd appear
In such a dreadful spot

She'd rather lose her balance
Her gowns, her gloves, her Art
She'll die denying it, of course
You won't believe me but I saw
Felicia shopping at K-Mart.

JYTTA

Is there anyone who's cuter
Than our dearest little Jytta?
If there is and you know her
Please show her
To me

Yes, I would be a suitor
For the lovely hand of Jytta
If I didn't have a wife
Who's the darling of my life
You see

If only she could be my tutor
That multi-talent wonder Jytta
I'd gladly burn the midnight oil
For my tutor I would toil
Incessantly

There's no one who's astuter
She is perfect, don't transmute her
Take your hats off, let's salute her
Here's a Happy Birthday, Jytta
I guarantee.

CAROLA

While watching Rachel and my girl cavort
Some twenty years ago one summer day
A garden statue twice as large as they
Fell off its seemingly secure support
That's how I first found out what a good sport
Carola is, for though a bloody spray
Enveloped all, without the least dismay
She listened on the phone to my report

Then raced across town with the speed of light
And kissed away the tears and washed the head
And calmed the last remaining waves of fright
And cleaned the garden steps where Rachel bled
And while the kids resumed their playful flight
We heard the ripples of their laughter spread.

SOFIA ELLA

I have a daughter named Bella
And one called Nicte-ha Osha
Now you've got Sofia Ella
I just hope that everything's kosher

Cause daughters are diamonds a dozen
More precious than all worldly gain
I keep a couple flash frozen
In a cryonic locker in Spain

So if ever I run out of daughters
Or find myself short one or two
I just have to ring up headquarters
And they'll instantly thaw out a few

And send them wherever I'm living
No matter what part of the world
For daughters are gifts worth the giving
Why be boyed when you can be girled?

MOTHER'S DAY

There is one friend among the rest who stands
Tall as a lily in a field that's rife
With countless weeds and thorns and shifting sands
Who for some decades now has shared my life
Her name is Linda with the lovely hands
She is my daughters' mother and my wife
To honor her in hopes she won't depart
For pain I've caused, I give her here my bleeding heart.

NICTE–HA

In that far land where all your dreams come true
I wandered searching for the fabled wealth
An ancient map described and told myself
Here's an endeavor worthy to pursue
And then, at last, when it came into view
After those years of intrigue, sweat and stealth
In which I lost my sanity and health
I found I'd made of nothing much ado

A thousand strands of pearls each richer, moister
Than the last one, their value not to be computed
And though each pearl seemed larger than the oyster
And their authenticity was undisputed
Somehow this fortune paled and lost its luster
What treasure, for a daughter's love, could be substituted?

DANNY

Danny, a little bird with golden wing
Whose image Guatemalans favor so
That they adorn their clothes, most everything
Their currency and art so that it show
This bird. This bird, whom they have made a king
With feathers green as a pistachio
Now flies its way to you but cannot sing
And in the silence of its form must show

How glad I am to celebrate with you
The anniversary of that event
When you leaped outward in astonishment
A small socialite making her debut
And here you are bigger, stronger, older
Your face a brilliant sun, brighter, golder.

GINGER

All of the guys try to hit on her
Each hoping to get his mitt on her
It's the way that her clothes fit on her
But it doesn't unhinge her

She's smooth enough to stand up under
Such attitudes, aloof as thunder
Cool and friendly, sometimes I wonder
If fire could singe her

One day while serving the sacred fruit
In wandered some despicable brute
Who, on noticing that she was cute
Thought he'd try to injure

That lady who brings the holy food
And elevates the general mood
On her serenity intrude
The wretched infringer

Now he's exiled to outer space
For daring to think he would debase
The aura and the stately grace
That surrounds sweet Ginger.

BETSY

Djordje, the gentle giant bear
Was shuffling thru this forest floor
I see his massive footprints here
And now I'm absolutely sure
Before the rising of the star
We'll find ourselves upon his door.

Look, there's the vast expanse of lawn
Where cottonwoods reach for the sky
The bear cubs tumbling up and down
Be careful, don't disturb their play
For just the breeze from one great paw
Can put a good sized man away.

Let's go inside, aromas call
And circulate throughout the cave
Intoxicating odors fill
The roomy den where these bears live
Let's see what's roasting on the grill
And let's observe how bears behave.

Today is special for the matriarch
The alpha female, mother bear, the queen
Who's celebrating fifty years of work
Since first she floated down upon the scene
For fifty years is a high water mark
She's halfway thru — and Betsy is her name.

She stands alone a moment in the crowd
As if she stood upon a desert shore
In regal splendor as a mother should
Did Gods give her as human gift to bears
Because she's so unutterably good
To wash away all trace of mortal cares?

Watch how her clan is circling about
With her as center, pivot, balance, hub
They form a monument in mammal suits
Complete — except do they need one more cub?
Lords of the western lands, great bears in boots
Who have invited us here to their club

To celebrate the famous fifty step
Upon the ladder that we all must climb
Rung after rung right from the bottom up
One foot immersed in splendor, one in slime
Let's all drink from the birthday loving cup
That turns us animals to things sublime.

THREE DAUGHTERS

I have three lovely daughters
And though I'm not a King
My daughters all are Princesses
You ought to hear them sing:

"I need a hat to match my dress,
A feather for my hat,
And then a jeweled hummingbird
To sit on top of that."

"I want a golden stallion,
A saddle made of pearl
With fringes dripping diamonds."
That's my youngest girl.

"I need, I want, I've got to have
I must, I really must
These rings, these things, and these and quick
Before I turn to dust."

A tropic cruise, to start the day
The middle one would please
A crystal swan, the eldest says,
Would set her mind at ease.

And then they laugh and cry and play
Or whine and primp and pee
Or sulk, cajole, make shopping lists,
And climb all over me.

Contemporary Princesses
I'd trade them for no other
My daughters three – but two of them
Call the oldest Mother.

THE DUCHESS

I used to hang around those spots
Where debutantes would moor their yachts,
And lounge on Persian rugs
I'd only smoke the stuff or sniff
Because it made me feel as if
I didn't need no drugs.

In fact, I spent a lot of time
Between the verses and the rhyme
Outright womanizing.
I found those legs, those thighs, those hips,
Eurasian and Venusian lips,
Much too appetizing

To ever think I had enough.
I'd lie around all day en buff
In some palatial suite —
The Hotel Mons, The Hotel Loins —
And stroke the lovely ladies' groins,
Rosette and Marguerite,

Ramona, Eunice, Babs and Flo —
Girls from the archipelago,
A sister of two queens,
A pair of twins who knew the ropes
(Gazelles among the antelopes)
And several dozen teens.

I never needed a translator
To speak to girls from the Equator,
The Andes or the Rhine,
If niceties we need distinguish
I'd talk away in body English.
There was a Florentine ...

A Duchess— I remember now
We met upon the strand somehow
She turned her head real quick
Her gown was lapis lazuli
She certainly was shocked when I
Performed the cigarette trick.

I'd lay a lighted cigarette
Along my finger tops and let
The burning end stick out
No more than just a tiny bit;
Then with the other hand I'd hit
My back-palm and I'd shout:

"I never miss," and with these words,
As elegant as flights of birds
Migrating to the South,
The burning cigarette would leap
(Slim acrobat aroused from sleep)
And flip into my mouth!

Take it from me, it's quite a show,
You can't believe the way girls go
Into a kind of fit!
There's something 'bout a cigarette
Describing arcs that makes them sweat
And instantly submit

To flattery or a caress.
Right here she's taking off her dress
It's down around her hips,
Her thighs, her legs. With an embrace,
The Duchess, in a public place,
Deftly, my pants unzips

They have a way, the very rich
No matter where they are, an itch
Must instantly be scratched;
On the streets, in a museum,
Taking pleasure, Carpe Diem!
The moment must be snatched.

We danced through Florence, Rome, Milan
I took her to the Vatican
(She made me do it there).
We checked into a French Dude Ranch
She did it in an avalanche
With someone named Pierre.

In Sicily: the volcano
While watching all that lava flow,
One night in Syracuse,
So overcome by her great thirst,
She got a publisher named Hearst
To help her reproduce—

He thought— a series of novellas.
But after several tarantellas,
Her meaning became clear
As long as she could find a mate,
She was content to fecundate
Across the hemisphere.

Her appetites were strange and vast.
She must have spent some time in past
Lives as a courtesan
Some royal concubine who learned
The proper way a trick is turned
For the Emperor of Japan

Or for a Sultan, an Emir
She did it strictly for the sheer
Unimaginable
Pleasure that it always brought her.
She was Aphrodite's daughter
Running after trouble,

Which she found at every corner.
When a brutal love had torn her
Into shreds and patches,
She'd crystallize into her stance
And rush out seeking high romance
At the Polo matches.

We had a boat in Mexico
She borrowed from an Eskimo
Who came there for the races.
She found it cozy on her back
When upside down in his kayak
She'd put me through the paces.

She left me when we reached the coast.
Exhausted, drained, pale as a ghost
I woke to find her gone.
I'll need a lifetime to recover
From such an energetic lover
As my Duchess-Amazon.

JANET RENO

Justice, Janet, absolutely
Just don't act irresolutely
By mistake have them execute me
For that would be a crime
Mercy-tempered-justice, Janet,
Letter, spirit, carved in granite
Raise the living level of the planet
Life screams: Now is the time!

Justice can be so demanding
Wisdom, knowledge not withstanding
In a universe that's still expanding
Why is justice blind?
Not blind. Too sad. The band she wears
Around her eyes reflects the stares
Of Justice seekers worn away with cares
Be merciful, be kind.

Justice can be visionary
Note one judge's commentary:
"If you can't be just, be arbitrary."
I swear that's what he said.
While law's delay is out of line
And just desserts on the decline
Poetic justice is, I know, divine
Unless I've been misled.

Revenge's a dish that's best served cold
But retribution smells of mold
Pour sparkling Freedom we can taste and hold
Justice, Janet, serve it hot!
It is the perfect antidote.
Your time and energy devote
To those poor souls, no matter how remote,
Whom justice has forgot.

DAYNI

If I should ever throw a fit
Because I find a cherry pit
Floating in my hot chocolate
I just hope that Dayni

Is there to comfort me and mop
My brow and make the madness stop
With mounds of whipped cream piled on top
Beautiful and brainy

She glides like an ambassador
From kitchen thru the garden door
A half a foot above the floor
So perfectly zany

Are the sparkles of her laughter
Reaching right up to the rafter
They penetrate to the hereafter
And change a dark and rainy

Washed-out morning dismal and slick
By some sort of magical trick
Into a comfortable old time flick
Black and white and grainy.

RICKY

When mother died the Rabbi said
Now that both your parents are dead
Max and Betty who bore and bred
The two of you from scratch

You must realize the state you're in
You're orphans now thru thick and thin
You are each other's only kin
And must begin from scratch

Orphans — the word hit me a belt
Like Ali throws, at once I felt
My heart congeal, my senses melt
An itch you couldn't scratch

But he was right, we were the last
Surviving members of a past
That turned to present much too fast
And we could hardly catch

Our breath before we were alone
Our Mom and Dad slipped off, were gone
And Rick and I became less two, more one
Starting each day from scratch.

A SPANISH TOAST

Penelope — that picture is so hot
Riding a bike in your forget me not
Dumbstruck just like a tongue-tied polyglot
I stood and wondered where

Exactly was that winding mountain road
And thought that if all day such traffic flowed
I'd buy some land and build a small abode
And live my life right there

I'd look off at the distant mountain peaks
And when from outside I'd hear bicycle squeaks
I'd rush out to admire those passing cheeks
The bifurcated pear

That jauntily bestrides the tiny seat
The pumping thighs, the calves, the pedaling feet
A centaur woman, bike and body meet
And I can only stare

And recall thru the hum of cicadas
That splendid Spanish toast: "Amor, pesetas
Y mujeres en bicicletas"
A toast, and yes, a prayer

And recall thru heat that melts icicles
That splendid Spanish toast to thricycles:
"Love, money and women on bicycles"
A toast, and yes, a prayer.

ALICE

While chewing on life's bitter rind
And swamped with troubles of all kind
I dream of gardens in my mind
And stare out at the sky

The world's too much a misery
For any one to always see
The nature of its harmony
Too hard to even try

Enveloped in this foul mood
In agonizing solitude
On universal woe I brood
Until I start to cry

Then suddenly my tears stop flowing
I'm back in tune with gardens growing
And once again life's easy going
And here's the reason why:

From the hands of Alice Parrot
Comes a dish bright red as claret
Topped with whipped cream, to my garret
Home made strawberry pie.

ZULIE

From the taut strings of the cello
Come a vibrant, muted bellow
Golden, haunting, ageless, mellow
Earthy as Jamaica

Like the harbinger, the crocus
She springs up in the circle's locus
Wearing a mask, for perfect focus,
Of lavender nacre

A hush descends, we hold our breath
As this vision of Ashtoreth
Laughs right into the face of Death
That grim undertaker

Her dance invokes the spirit rising
Creative urge uncompromising
Forever new, always surprising
Delicate earth shaker

Her hands and fingers hold the answer
Arms and legs of the enchanter
All the movements of the dancer
Twinkle-toed Zuleika.

KATHELIN

I was an ordinary kid
I swung on gates, I ran and hid
I did whatever was forbid
To pass the live-long day

I grew up in the forties when
War was the normal way of men
Until the bombs of hydrogen
Made everything decay

The world reshaped into a place
Unjubilant and vile and base
Devoid of any touch of grace
Designed just to dismay

But I remember how I'd wake
Without a care when day would break
Back then when life was still a piece of cake
And mornings made for play

I'd jump from bed and I would soar
Right thru life's starry corridor
With someone like whom this small poem's for
Dear Miss Kathelin Gray.

CAROLA

Tossed like a salad, like a boat
From wave to crashing wave we float
Abandoned, desperately remote
'Til on an unknown shore

Washed up, in fairylands forlorn
World-weary, foot-sore, weather-worn
Our body pierced, belabored, torn
We gasp upon death's-door

And struggle with the endless strife
Sharp thorns rebuffing our dull knife
And drag ourself thru what's called life
'Til an ambassador

Who seems as scattered as we are
But actually an Avatar
As steady as the morning-star
Will pleasant times restore

With the just the nature of her being
With her soft touch, with her clear-seeing
Heavenly harmony decreeing
Carola evermore.

DECHEN

Right in the middle of a painful throe
My mind and body at an all time low
Quite sure that I not one more step could go
The telephone began to ring

With that insistent sound you can't ignore
I dragged myself across the parlor floor
Like answering a knock upon death's-door
At once all hope abandoning

I picked the damn thing up, I had no choice
And heard the softest, sweetest, kindest voice
Whose lilting southern tone made me rejoice
Glad again just to be living

You knew first hand what I was going through
Having yourself strolled down that avenue
Your voice, your words were able to renew
Like a magic wand, my being

And now, Dechen, that perfect sixtieth year
Reveals her secret music to your ear
And I rejoice again that I am here
To sing this song to you this evening.

TWO DAUGHTERS

One of my daughters' a Buddhist
She sits on the path and recites
Mantras that float to the heavens
And practices Buddhistic rites

One of my daughters' a Nudist
Though not always stripped to the skin
She practices forms of Nudistics
Both bask in the sun from within.

MY FATHER

My father told me long ago
So many things that I was slow
In appreciating
His words of wisdom down the drain
He warned me not to eat chow mein
And to stop masturbating!

So I ate plenty Chinese food
To spite his holy attitude
Because it was denied,
And constantly would yank my wang
I knew the thrill, the swoon, the pang
But neither satisfied

My appetites, they'd merely tease.
To masturbate, eat food Chinese,
Those pleasures I'd pursue.
Great bowls of shrimp chow mein devour,
Then drop my fruitless passion flower
That's all I'd ever do!

But soon, to my complete distress,
A sudden hollow emptiness
Would take me at the door.
Your belly's full one minute past,
And then, as if fresh from a fast,
You've got to eat some more!

The same with pulling on your tool
The photo-flash is almost cruel,
So transient and fleeting.
One second, heaven welcomes you,
Then, up the creek with no canoe
Whacking off and eating.

Then wisdom pointed out the truth.
I learned as I played out my youth,
I might as well have eaten
The grease burger, with melted cheese,
Chow mein, it seems, is as Chinese
As Einstein is a cretin!

And that affair with Damsel Hands
(As well as countless one-night stands
With every kind of mate)
Was fun, like bogus Chinese meals
But now it's abalone, eels!
And I'm a graduate

Of certain secret sexual schools
We concentrate on molecules
Until the body faints.
Our policy is to abstain;
We store our seed inside the brain
And, much like yogic saints

We never let our fluid drop
To breed a Golden Gully crop,
But rather let it rise
Along the spinal circuitry
Until it nestles perfectly
Right there, behind the eyes.

So both things that he warned me of:
Chicken chow mein, one-handed love,
Turned out empty pockets.
A burst of flame, taste buds explode
Before you know you've shot your load
Pancaked, burnt-out rockets.

Yes, Dad was right again, it seems.
I'm glad he never forbade dreams,
Because at just that time
I dreamed unto the maximum,
Sweet dreams, a whole compendium
And usually in rhyme.

BARRY MASSIN

He's handling sixteen guys at once
A normal day performing stunts
There's twenty more on hold
But all of them are wearing smiles
While Barry jogs four-minute miles
They must have broke the mold

After they saw this chap display
His skill in steel, papier mache
And everything between
When one is so superabundant
A dozen more would be redundant
He must burn gasoline

Instead of blood inside his veins
While juggling worlds he entertains
I know a God he ain't,
But watch him in his studio
His workshop-castle, then you'll know
He's half machine, half saint.

HEBREW ZEN MASTER

A celebrated simpleton
Who searched the world and finding none
Of all the things he sought,
Asked a Jewish gentleman
Or was it a monk from Japan?
If knowledge could be bought.

He asked why Jews, or Nipponese
Were just as smart as you could please.
The answer: "Herring heads
For just a couple bucks a throw,
You'll be completely in the know,
You'll lecture to the Feds."

So, every day this chap would pop
Into the oriental shop,
Buy fish heads from the Jew,
Until one day he stopped to think,
Poised upon enlightenment's brink,
He thought he really knew.

He raced across town to the store;
The Yiddish Jap stood by the door
"How come I pay two bucks
For herring heads? Am I so dense
The whole fish costs just fifty cents!
Are we goys sitting ducks"

Inscrutable, the Jews, the Japs
Known for never caught taking naps,
The answer came out steady:
"Hold on, my friend, I'm not a crook,
The money is not lost, just look!
You're getting smarter already."

WIVES

How nice we are to our friends' wives
How truly heartfelt nice
As if we're nice all thru our lives
And never even once threw knives
At our own little wife.

SANTA FE

They ask me everywhere I go
What things are like in Mexico.
"New Mexico," I say.
How do you pass the time out there
In San Jose, does it compare ...?
"No, No! It's Santa Fe!"

Well, We lie around all day in splendor,
Ambrosia, nectar in the blender,
On terraced mountain tops
Like Gods in pearl encrusted boots,
We speak only in absolutes
And pull out all the stops.

Hop in your car and drive out there
Stars swim in pools of crystal air
You're in for a surprise:
The welcome station knows your name
They're overjoyed, so glad you came
They even know your size!

Yes, spread upon the desert lawn
Your own pearl boots, your own new sawn
Off shotgun, and for luck
Old turquoise beads, a western hat
Coors beer, string tie, a lariat
And brand new pick-up truck.

They give you maps, a few stiff shots,
Some priceless Pueblo Indian pots
And send you on your way
Along that road so charming, quaint,
Where there's no need to feel restraint
The trail to Santa Fe,

The open skies, the endless plain,
Highway rest stops that serve champagne,
The cactus silhouette
That dominates the distant hills
And then without fanfare or frills,
One more perfect sunset

As you go roaring down the road
But, wait! That car ahead has slowed
He signals like a gent,
He's pulling in, you'd better stop
A combination litter drop
And Historic Monument

Is coming up — don't think I mock,
This grand affair (like Camel Rock)
Is something you must see.
Look! Ancient writing on the cliff;
Stop here, my friends, especially if
You have to take a pee.

It's Paradise, I won't be vague
Land of the Flea, Home of the Plague
The cozy Great Southwest.
Smart dinner clubs, Art without reason,
Prison riots, the Opera Season…

SUSHI JOCKEY

Let's dine, my friends, let's have a feast
And drink the mythological beast
Kirin Beer and sake
Served up with a gigantic dish
Of raw, delicious, fresh-sliced fish
By the sushi jockey.

Now, here's the only food that works!
For while a hundred million jerks
Are dining out on beef,
Those fellows with the almond eyes
Have planned another sea-surprise,
Fresh from the coral reef.

Yes, this rosette is salmon pale,
Arranged between some yellow-tail.
That orange splash is roe.
Do they eat like this on Luna?
King clam, octopus and tuna
Tied with a seaweed bow

Red snapper is sliced paper-thin,
Pink abalone, dark bluefin,
Bay scallops stuffed in nests
Of snails and eels, and to my shame,
Some purple item I can't name
Let's dine, my honored guests!

INGRATE

Ingratitude's so much a part
Of human nature that it's smart
To take it for granted,
Not to be hurt, to understand
"Thank yous" are fine in Wonderland
Where everyone's enchanted

But in this world the very least
You might expect from your fellow beast
In the way of gratitude
Is just about what he'll express
The very least, or a little less
You know the attitude.

OCCULT ADULT

Well, you can fast for forty days
Or contemplate a Chinese vase
Or raise your arms above
Your head and hold them there all year
'Til visions come and disappear,
Or concentrate on love,

Or prayers, or deeds, the blessed kind
Suspend the functions of your mind
In amniotic tanks,
Or practice varied magic arts,
Probe deep into your heart of hearts,
And simply draw blanks.

Or try yogic postures, tantric twists,
Enveloping yourself in mists
Of marijuana smoke
All are effective to a point;
Right now I'm lighting up a joint
And hoping I don't choke

On special diets, sleepless nights,
The ancient rituals and rites,
The thousand different modes
Designed to elevate the soul,
To bring it nearer to its goal
Before the thing corrodes,

Becomes a rusted entity,
A thing without identity.
There's hardly any chance
A breakthrough will occur before
You turn into a total boor
And need an ambulance

To rush you from the scene to spare
Your friends from having mal-de-mer
And not even a pill
To save them from that awful motion
When you get stuck on some new notion,
Why, everyone gets ill!

So just relax and take a bath.
There is a way to find the path,
To open up the door.
Remember this: some way, somehow,
Things are more like they are right now
Than they ever were before!

POETS AND ATOMIC ARTISTS
Tony Price

An artist down in Santa Fe
Who turns out pieces night and day
Whose life's example shows the way
For many on the path
Is grinning at a private joke
Which came to him just as he woke
And now he's looking for a smoke
To take into the bath.

Here every room is jammed with art
All fashioned with his hand and heart
To find your way you'd need a chart
It flows into the yard
A solid mass of art so dense
Thank God the place has got a fence
Or this outrageous opulence
Would fill the boulevard.

It's morning and the world's in shreds
It makes men jump back in their beds
The covers pulled over their heads
To keep away the dawn.
The artist grins and rises up
He brews the coffee, finds the cup
He drinks and smokes and pets the pup
While wondering what to pawn.

But nothing here is worth the dust
Or worth a little flake of rust
No, not a crumb, not worth a crust
At the pawnbroker's shop.
Out there you need something that's real
To have a chance to make a deal
A watch, a suit, something you steal,
Not art or some such slop.

Poets and atomic artists
Make the maps, they are the chartists
And among the very smartest
Life-forms in the crowd
Focusing an inward vision,
Clearing vistas with precision,
On a course without collision
Quiet, they speak out loud.

Though doomed to poverty they're blessed,
Unrecognized among the rest,
Unknown, they pass the hardest test.
Each day they blaze a trail
Alone through unexplored terrain
Ignoring pleasure, bearing pain
Spilling their life-blood from each vein
While to the stars they sail.

STROKE

Tony Price

A lightning flashes in the sky
And splits the atmosphere in half
Peels back the veil, reveals the way
And no one sees it but yourself.
A stroke of lightning hits the flesh
And sends the body in a slide
Two limbs, a mind, the rest all ash
So stricken no one dares to trade

His place with you, to take that ride.
It's harder than exchanging blood
To switch your cloaks of living dread
And try each other on inside
Where organs roar and tissues flood
And colors all are shades of red.

THE DREAM

Look! Tony's riding on a horse
Along a river to its source
He's driven by some driving force
Which keeps him on the go

The jungle swoops down to the shore
And covers up the forest floor
But he knows every wall's a door
And moves on with the flow

Caught in a mighty monsoon's wrath
The river washes out the path
Swamps them in a torrential bath
A dreadful undertow

Look! Tony's swimming up the stream
Deep in his eye a distant gleam
Chasing the impossible dream
His face, in dark, aglow

The river swerves around a bend
He disappears and I pretend
He's swimming still, swim on, my friend
Swim on, and Westward ho!

ART THERAPIST

I am a Therapist of Art
All matters of the head and heart
Of tissue, blood and soul
I leave to learned medicos
Whose mysteries I won't expose
Since I'm out on parole.

I've found the way to separate
The spirit from the packing crate
And for this I was debarred,
Unfrocked and drummed out of the corps
Humiliated (and for an encore)
I was feathered and tarred.

The only problem that I cure
Is how to make Fine Art endure
No matter what it takes
I diagnose the frail and weak
Unspeakable human physique
And never make mistakes.

I have prescribed excessive drink
To keep some patients in the pink
In shape for making Art
I'll meddle in their private life
Calm down, frustrate, infuriate a wife,
A mistress, a sweetheart.

I disregard the dreadful ache
That Artists feel — for their Art's sake
For when the moment strikes
And Art comes pouring out in reels
It doesn't matter how the artist feels
What he thinks or likes

As long as he's creating work
That is supreme— insane, berserk,
Who cares— happy, sad or smart!
In fact, I often recommend
Suicide as the perfect end
'Cause Death will further his Art.

COUNT ALBERT CARLO

Now is the time for courage, lads
We have eluded phases, fads,
Nothing we can't surmount.
Ignore the fever, pain, the ache,
One mile more and then we take
Refreshment with The Count.

I used to cheer the men this way
To get them through another day
I'd breathe into them life
With just a word about the man
Or stories of his master plan,
Forget about your wife

If you could spend the night instead
Gazing at Albert Carlo's head
Across the coffee table,
And disappear into the weave
Of tales he'd tell, real, make-believe
If only we were able

To relish for eternity
The pleasure of his company,
To freeze Time in its track,
To concentrate our energy
On this one task — If only we
Could bring Count Carlo back

These days, each morning I can find
Him strolling leisurely through my mind.
Sometimes he tips his hat.
He's dressed in tails or cloth of gold,
Sometimes he's young, sometimes he's old,
I see him when we met,

A dapper fellow, every inch
Nobility, with just a pinch
Of pepper from the street.
With massive head and jet-black beard
Larger than life The Count appeared,
So trim, so slim, so neat.

I often see him sailing through
A river in a bark canoe,
Wearing a sombrero.
I see him on the boulevards
Or at the tables, playing cards,
Counting his dinero.

This master of the perfect scam
Was on his way to Amsterdam
To see the flowers bloom;
But changed his mind and took the deep
Long ride into eternal sleep
And checked into a room

With hot and cold running jazz.
A room with everything. He has
A view of all the world.
His art, his pens and pads are stacked,
If trouble comes, his bags are packed.
And in it Carlo's curled

Up in a cozy little nook
Reading or writing in a book,
Or working in his lab
To let us know that things are fine.
Soon as he can he'll send a sign,
Plane tickets and a cab.

You who have known The Count and spoke
With him, and shared a drink or smoke
Remember if you can,
You actually were talking with
More of a legend or a myth
Than a mere mortal man.

Remember if you can
How many women exhausted, return?
How many ladies can that satyr mount?
How many lovers revive and re-burn?
How many girls have gone down for The Count?

GOOD BUDDY

I've kept a secret for some time
Embarrassment, not lack of rhyme
Has made my mouth a seal.
It is the con man's lucky break
That marks are too ashamed to wake
The world with their appeal.

But when your pal, your trusted friend,
Your partner who's supposed to send
You money that he owes,
Calls up to say he's goin' to steal
Your share (of course he puts it real
Nicely — he even shows

The reason why he can't refuse
Some deal, the details would confuse
Me — it just looks so good)
So he's taking all the money,
Shipping out to somewhere sunny,
I'd rather that some hood

Bitter, maddened from the ghetto
Press the point of his stiletto
Right up against my throat,
Demand I give him everything
The watch, the credit cards, the ring,
Even my overcoat.

But when this "pal" may his tubes rust
Exercises his wanton lust
Not only on the girls
But on the cash he held — for shame
I cannot hesitate to name
This swine who stole my pearls,

This vagrant cad who's done a few
Ultra-insidious deeds unto
Most everyone I know,
Now that I check around a bit.
I find the fellow's only fit
For making gardens grow,

If you get my inner meaning.
I'll drop him in a vat where cleaning
Powder's manufactured;
I'll push him off the window sill,
Mix up concrete, but not until
Several limbs are fractured!

I must reveal his name to save
Other victims from this knave.
I'll make of him fair game!
I'll tell the world about the guy
This slime, this filth is called —
But, why immortalize his name?

SMOKER

Like bacteria introduced
To septic systems long misused
To gobble up the sludge,
The food you think is passing through
Is actually eating you,
If I am any judge.

But have no fear that you'll expire
Decomposition's stopped by fire,
And now the meal is done:
A cheroot on the verandah.
Don't believe that propaganda
Smoking is really fun.

Yes, even as I write this line
I'm yielding to a genuine
Never-to-be-denied
Desire so implacable,
So primal it's untrackable,
A truly bona fide

Need to reach into my pockets,
Twist my arms from out their sockets
If that's the only way
To get that precious pack of smokes
Into my hands, have a few pokes,
Savor the rich bouquet

Of Turkish and Havana blend
Allow me, please, to recommend
That taste upon the tongue —
Tobacco. Raleigh said: "Divine",
That relaxation of the spine
And ecstasy of lung.

I want to drop my fountain pen
And smoke a cigarette again,
Some sweet Virginia leaf.
Can anything in life replace
That hot, voluptuous embrace
The agonized relief

Of lighting up a cigarette,
Positioning that minaret
Just right between the lips,
To suck the fiery mouthfuls in,
To puff that smoking javelin
And feel the mild whips

Of fire dancing in the throat.
There's only one known antidote—
And that's: to have another.
The spiral curls of smoke erase
All memory of pain, disgrace
In smoke I'd rather smother

Than rot away behind a desk,
Become a thing half barbaresque
Deprived of my fresh pack,
Unnerved, unjubilant, unclean
Quite useless without nicotine,
The thrice divine tabac.

When I'm struck with a brilliant thought
I thank the Lord my carton's bought
And in the cabinet.
Just knowing that ten packs are there
Relieves the tension in the air
I swear, a cigarette

Enhances every single act
The most mundane, the most abstract
And you can make a bet,
To lend grace, enthusiasm,
To avoid a daily spasm,
I'll need a cigarette!

Sometimes although I puff and puff
I feel I haven't had enough,
And since I'm not a dunce,
I'll pull a handful from the pack
And, like a pyromaniac,
Light them all up at once.

So what, if there's a little taste
Of mucilage, library paste,
A hint of Elmer's glue?
Who cares if they're a little stale
When you are longing to inhale,
They're sweet as honeydew.

Far sweeter, now I think on it
I hope I never have to quit
(Like ordinary saps
Chew gum and bite my fingernails)
The kind of pleasure smoke unveils
Is made for special chaps.

When Trace-Purcell was asked to stop
By members of the Club who'd hop
Upon his case all day,
Rehearse the toxic side effects,
Hereditary birth defects,
The price he'd have to pay

For filling up his lungs with smoke,
The dangers of a fatal stroke,
He'd swear it smacked of theft:
"Damn funny business, old chaps
Put my tobacco under wraps
And I'll have nothing left!"

THE BWANA'S CLUB

Trace-Purcell

God, Ex-Commander Trace-Purcell!
We knew each other very well
If one can know another.
We saved each other's lives in spite
Of fear, which makes betrayal bright-
Er than skin of blood-brother.

One morning, hot upon the trail
Of wildebeest, he seemed to fail
He turned and asked me if
I thought the applications of
Mustachio wax below, above
Still held his mustache stiff

He thought it drooped a bit, perhaps
And then he started burning maps
To get the water hot
Enough to shave, right on the track
Wildebeest breathing down our back
I gave it my best shot

And held the mirror to his face.
Master of the leisurely pace,
He dawdled through his shave;
And I suppose that if I fell
Head first in quicksand, pits of Hell,
He'd just as quickly save

My life as I did his. You see,
Action, Despair, and Unity's
The motto of our Club.
It's just good form and no wonder
When a member's going under
To un-stopper the tub!

As long as there's a shred of hope,
Just throw a Bwana enough rope,
And if he doesn't sprain
An ankle, break a leg, some gang
Of Sherpas from the hills will hang
Him with it. Or a train

Will slice the worthy chap in halves
While he's admiring the calves
Of girls who're looking cool.
Expeditions to the jungle
Are not the time or place to bungle
That's a Bwana's Club rule.

The last I ever saw of him
Was disappearing round the rim
Two hundred feet below,
Straight downward and descending yet
Until his glowing cigarette
Was the only thing to show.

But he survived, so goes the tale,
Although I only heard the pale
Haggard story-teller
Reiterate that close escape
And then produce Trace's last tape,
Which contained a stellar

Performance of the Bwana's creed,
A list of animals that he'd
Discovered in the brush
(More mythological I'm sure
Than everyday big game that you're
Familiar with). I blush

Recounting what came next: a poem
Nay, several ones. That devilish gnome
Was talking onto tape
In some forgotten hidden spot,
Most likely more half-dead than not,
Inspired by the grape

Or native drink with which he liked
To have his whiskey-soda spiked,
Waxing sentimental
Just picture it: his ranger hat
Sways in the breeze, falls to the mat
With a sound as gentle

As unheard melodies are sweet.
The man ought to be making neat
Bundles of loose events,
Tying up ends, presenting facts
Recording views, reviewing acts
Instead of making dents

In that fragile, polished, tender
Vehicle whose brilliant fender
Is the King's own English
You'd think that those years in the bush
Had cured him of such school girl mush
Poetry is ticklish

In the best of circumstances
Poets move around in trances
And wander from the trail,
Yet here in some small palm-thatched hut
Our Trace-Purcell crushed out his butt
And told the final tale

In words super-charged with meaning.
The test for poetry is leaning
With all your inner ear
Against the poem as it comes through
A perfect one, out of the blue,
Will make you disappear!

And there it is — I ask, my friend,
Can you find a happier end?
The man realized his form,
His nature, being, life, his art
(Though penniless with a broken heart)
That image keeps him warm.

Succinct and pithy, to the point
He knew the time was out of joint;
He's picking up the stub
Of some fresh stepped-on cigarette,
It's raining and the streets are wet
Outside the Bwana's Club.

STEVE LACY

A quarter of a century
Has thrilled us with immensity
Since Trace-Purcell became
A member of the Bwana's Club,
His former life completely scrubbed,
Adopted his new name.

Those early years he used to hang
Around with a musician's gang,
His closest pal was Lacy.
They were fellows of a kidney,
Trace was Bix and Steve was Sidney
Look very hard, you may see

Their record made in fifty four,
Sutton was Trace's name then, for
The book. You should have heard
That music very few could hear
Insistent, agonized and clear
Trace was Miles, Lacy, Bird.

Then, shortly after, Trace gave up
The trumpet, cornet, muting cup,
Even the mellophone
Stretch the fabric, nothing's giving
There's no way to make a living
Seeking the perfect tone.

But, Lacy, from a different cut
Of cloth, cared nothing for the hut
Of thatch, the trapper's cage;
To wander the unbeaten tract
Was not his idea of an act,
He much preferred the stage,

The public eye and public ear.
Deep in the bush you cannot hear
Contemporary sound
Except the roaring of some beast,
So Lacy hung about the East
Coast and he played around

In tiny clubs, Bowery Five-spot,
The Blue Note, Half Note, le jazz hot
Montmartre, Riviera
To name a few of those quaint dives;
That period in memory thrives:
New York Primavera

When Hawk sat in with Al Bandini
(A mismatch like Ben Mussolini
And Joe DiMaggio)
But nobody was finding work
Not even as a soda jerk,
No less quartet or trio.

So off Lacy went to Paris
To the perpetual embarrass-
Ment of the U.S.A.
Find it strange to see a master
Of the arts who's nourished faster
A continent away

Than on his own native soil?
Our policy is not to spoil
The artist on the fringe.
Remember how the Living Theater
Was hounded from the U.S. clear to
Europe. It makes you cringe!

And then we shamefully request
Years late: "Come back, as honored guest."
And so it came about
That Lacy, an expatriate
For decades now, finds himself fit
To have another bout

In old New York (new wave and punk)
To honor and interpret Monk
For just a couple days.
And suddenly by chance or choice
I'm poking through the Village Voice
And what should meet my gaze?

But an ad, an advertisement
For the general apprisement
Of every citizen
To say: Lacy et al's in town,
A string of pearls to deck the crown
Of Monk. I grab my pen,

I jot the number on the wall
And after making one quick call,
We're talking on the phone
Now, twenty years have passed since I've
Seen him or heard his music strive
For mastery of tone.

We talk a bit, of this, of that,
"A million things to do," we chat
And then I sort of sigh:
"I'm working on an epic song"
A pause, and then he says: "Sounds long,"
And then we say, "Good-bye."

Well, I guess he really ought to know
For next week on the radio
A Lacy marathon
Is starting up, all set to go,
It runs for NINETY hours or so
But Lacy, he's long gone

To Paris. Day and night, it runs
While moons and stars and setting suns
Revolve throughout the sky;
But Lacy, he's in Paris-town,
His music tipped me upside-down
And nearly made me cry.

In twenty years a lot of things
Go down and what the future brings
Is always a surprise;
I think I'd rather throw my lot
With famous unknown artists, not
Commercial enterprise.

With Bellavia, Price, with Trace,
Art is the gnome, your life, the chase.
So Lacy, let us try
To meet again sometime before
Another twenty years or more
Go plunging headlong by.

And maybe we can mix it up,
Invite the Muse in for a cup,
And if she brings my pen
And if you play a tune right through
My words, around, between, unto
We'll ask her in again!

FRANK SINATRA

Of all the things you could desire,
The heights to which you might aspire,
From Alphas to Omegas,
The power of wealth, looks like Apollo,
Youth, joy, peace — I'd like to follow
Sinatra at Las Vegas!

'Cause there's an act that's hard to follow.
Dancers choke and comics swallow
Upon the very rare
Occasions when it might fall out
(A benefit, a drinking bout,
Some special billionaire,

A marathon for cardiacs)
Where many, many dozen acts
Perform in random order,
So that someone who'd normally flank,
Would actually follow Frank!
And this poor sap would sorta

Stand there through eight or nine encores,
Stuck in the wings, while the applause
Seemed to go on forever.
Then Frank would leave the stage at last,
Accompanied by a final blast
Of cheers, and then you never

Heard a silent hush drop so hard
As everybody on the card
The entire audience
Sat on the edges of their seat
Like victims planted in concrete
And waited in immense

Expectation for the event,
Feeling the exquisite torment
Of him who's scheduled next,
Who'd have to pull one from his hat,
Some miracle to follow that
Performance beyond text.

Yes, if I had to make a choice
Between the Body and the Voice
(And that's no easy trick),
Making love to Cleopatra
Or to follow Frank Sinatra,
You know which one I'd pick!

SWEET TOOTH

I've just raced home across the bridge,
Take off my coat, start towards the fridge
And I spot the neighbor
Stuffing my wife — up to the hilt
My box of chocolate bon-bons on the quilt
This calls for the saber

To clear the air of what might be
Misconstrued as unneighborly,
My wife, my bed, my brandy,
I mean, a friendly visit during lunch
Is rectified with one swift punch
But — when they eat my candy!

CHOPPER

I took a Yugoslavian freighter
From New York to Tangier some years ago
I saw a meteor create a crater
And must admit it was quite a show
I watched police arrest a masturbator
For killing a potential embryo
Caught in this act illegal and improper
In his own garden, spotted by a helicopter.

HEALTHY DAVE

Fed up with French atrocity
Bored by nouvelle pomposity
Sick of Tex-Mex ferocity
That tastes like plastic wood?
There is a restaurant of renown
The one and only place in town
Where you can toss a great meal down
And walk out feeling good.

It's not a sushi bar I mean
It's not the Purple Nectarine
Italian, Chinese, Thai cuisine
That fill the neighborhood.
They won't be serving lobster tail
No tongues of hummingbird or quail
You can't get terrapin or snail
That much is understood.

It takes a lot of bravery
To dine where food's unsavory
Tired of dining slavery?
If so, my friends, you should
Take my advice to the gourmet
And save your stomach from decay
Go eat at Healthy Dave's Cafe!
I'd eat|there if I could.

JOHN DOMONT

It's appalling and astounding
It's enthralling and confounding
I'm 'a falling on the grounding
Up the creek with no canoe.

I was planning on attaining
An enchanting and sustaining
Magic fanning past explaining
When I went to visit you.

I was counting on carousing
At the fountain of your housing
And then mounting and arousing
Every single girl in view.

Sunday morning I'm relaxing
Heavy yawning is so taxing
Without warning my mind's faxing
Something I forgot to do.

I'm admitting that forgetting
Is only fitting for coquetting
And I'm sitting here regretting
That I missed your rendezvous.

LUCKY CHARM

I'm writing poems all day long
My mind and mouth are filled with song
I know that nothing can go wrong
Just the antitheses.

The words are flowing through my head
New images appear and spread
From what fresh fountains are they fed?
Is this some rare disease?

But there's no need to feel alarm
No way I'll ever come to harm
Long as I've got my lucky charm
Excuse me, I have to sneeze.

Oh lucky charm, you're now transferring
My words to print which keeps me purring
'Cause your computer speed is blurring
Don't need directories

To find someone who is unerring
With whom I find myself conferring
Indeed, at times, almost concurring
That madman, John DeVries.

ANDREW

Sometimes I see
Coming at me
Across the hall
Or off the wall
Bouncing along
Singing a song
A strange bundle
Of wonder
Smiling sundials
Of thunder
A perfect talent
With everything askew
A rag-tag gallant
Rolling down the avenue.

Sometimes he stops
And deftly pops
A hank of hair
With loving care
Under his hat.
His silk cravat
Adjusts, and then
Bounces away again.

Sartorial debauchee
With a hole at each knee
A breeze catches
Flapping patches
Dashing image maker
Half dada and part Quaker
Jeans are faded
Well aerated
Green bandanna
Xzentrekiana.

Clothes make the man
Some dapper-Dan
Insists, but I say no!
No suit or smart chapeau
On a man's body grows
I say: man makes the clothes.

TRACE–PURCELL

I think of Trace-Purcell flat on his back
In hospital. He thought some fast food snack
Responsible for the extreme distress
That clutched his gut and left him comfortless.
Quite broke but having honorably served
In war he hoped to get what he deserved
And staggered to the Hospital of Vets
Grease burgers, Hershey bars and cigarettes
His sole diet, provided the answer
A smashing case of colon cancer
Which surgeons, opening him up, soon found
To floriferously throughout abound.

No more than six weeks later he was dead
Never once having gotten out of bed
And seeing no one but his Mom and Sis
Only months afterwards we learned of this
He never contacted a single friend
Not wanting to intrude with his untimely end
Upon the living, or not knowing how
To break such news, perhaps he made a vow
Being the total and consummate loner
That when death the annuler and dethroner
Appeared he'd need no other chaperone
As usual it would be easier alone.

In fact his mother never even knew
When his spirit from that cage, that crate withdrew
They told her he recovered, took a trip
By then her memory started to slip
Well over ninety years; senility
Wrapped her in its divine tranquility.
He asked his sister at the very last
To call or write a few friends from the past
To let them know, after the soul passed thru him
I did not hear from her, I who knew him
So well, it made me think this is a cue
From Trace who purposely did not get thru
To me, and since in death I did not view him
Perhaps he wants me to find out what really happened to him

SEVERN DARDEN

On Heather's birthday last were you possessed?
Dressed up like Hillary on Everest
With high boots, oxygen, stout walking stick, a vest
I must say I was quite impressed
It was as if you stood there half undressed

Without a necktie blazing on your chest.
From all the glories of the world you chose the best
Placed yourself under house arrest
You leaped the threshold of your quest
And then in sweet surrender evanesced.

Now you're preserved forever in our minds
A symbol of the best of times
Your spirit flows in us like wine
And we are drunk trying to find
A meaning in this voyage up the line.

CHARLES BELL

If I could live as long and half as well
As that most lively man— my friend Charles Bell
And if I knew that this was guaranteed
And from all future effort I'd be freed
I'd lay my pen down and my bloody sword
Instead of being boring I'd be bored
Instead of fighting for each desperate cause
I'd patch old poems with bandages and gauze
And lie about the house and smoke my pipe
And gorge myself on caviar and tripe
And dream that if I lived four times as well
As man was meant to do that would be swell
Yes, life would be completely free of snarls
If I could live just twice as long as Charles.

ON FIRST VIEWING C.G. BELL'S "SYMBOLIC HISTORY"

Convoke, call a consistory
To solve this subtle mystery
How can Symbolic History
Not be much better known?

By luck, while scanning through the set
Through channels of despair, regret
Inanity, sex, bood and sweat
The tube threw me a bone

Before my eyes the patterns ran
Down channels measureless to man
Then stopped their passage in mid-scan
On something never shown

I saw the Grand Design unfold
Of man's creative spirit bold
At last the tale completely told
I watched. My mind was blown

This work will make the center hold
Yes, I felt chilly and grown old
From traveling in realms of gold
And sat there all alone.

ON FURTHER VIEWING C.G. BELL'S "SYMBOLIC HISTORY"

To dare
While riff-raff read rubbish
And declare
This stuff is really deep
To dare
While scholars grow sluggish
And watch each other fall asleep
To dare, I say
When such conditions prevail
To encompass all the world
Down to the last detail
And to serve up
Everything that matters
In golden cups
On well-wrought silver platters
So those who have acquired a taste
For immortality
Who recognize the pearl among the paste
May be refreshed by thee.

O 'tis a dare worth the daring
A labor, a care beyond caring
Great thanks for the bearing
Great thanks for sharing.

RUBIN

I've known a rolling Sumatran
Who barreled down the street
Like a hurricane meeting a mountain
On delicate dancing feet

I've known a lot of sparkling minds
Some quick and ready wits
I've seen guys handle orange rinds
And dig gigantic pits

I've heard the most outrageous sense of humor
And seen the most preposterous displays
Known men who worked despite a raging tumor
And didn't go to sleep for several days

I've watched men struggling with their art
And watched when art just flows
Like lava from the hand and heart
Until the artist glows

I've seen men charm the rings right off the fingers
Of fancy gals who thought they knew it all
Seen empty-handed men who still were bringers
Of greater cheer than any I recall

I've seen the most amazing men
Parading through my life
But Rubin, time and time again
Clears the air with a blast of oxygen
With a smile like a magic knife.

BRENT

I too have heard that lovely sixtieth year
Unfold her golden music in my ear
With warm affection and deep gratitude.
After six decades comes beatitude
A kind of gentle mysterious bliss
So that after reflecting on all this
This snake-like undulating trail from birth
Along the many-winding paths of earth

A sort of mellow overtone prevails.
On a lucky blue sky baronial white sails
Dissolve and smooth the passage into night
Hearts on fire, gathered in the fire-light
We toast each other with non-alcoholic beers
Sixty seconds, sixty minutes, sixty years.

LUKA

Now did you know that long ago, my lad
Your Daddy's Daddy's Daddy's Daddy's Dad
Would sail the seas thru weather good or bad
In a boat called a felucca

Way back in generations up the line
I see your ancestor in ancient time
Pluck on the strings and make music divine
Playing her sambouka

So many different genes mixed thru the ages
Starting from history's earliest pages
Combined their unique traits to make in stages
You — not some palooka

Only you sprung from joy and all things jolly
You alone born in the wild Wood of Holly
With roots from Yugoslavia to Bali
From the Land of the Yucca

And while you sleep the dream your mind is making
Becomes reality as you are waking
The whole wide world's out there for just the taking
If you want it, Luka.

ANDREW

Apart from a rollicking roll in the hay
Each glorious morning, each glorious day
And a few other pleasures along the way
I can't think of anything finer

Than to find that my mind has combined with another's
And we soar intertwined, in verse we are brothers
While we float unconfined past a world whose way smothers
The spirit of the Grand Designer.

ANDREW

I have survived all kinds of blows
Taken the best shots that life throws
Accepted all the slings, arrows
For richer and for poorer

I've traveled round the world and then
Retraced my journey once again
A universal citizen
I've watched life grow obscurer

I sought to find the noblest way
I gave my heart up to the play
Searched for the loveliest bouquet
Found Poetry was purer

I see the world now as it is
I know the nature of my biz
I watch the magic potion fizz
And nothing could be surer

I don't need an anesthetic
To wax instantly prophetic
Now that I've become poetic
Consultant to the führer

NOAH

Long, long ago in Paradise
God sent a serpent to entice
Man and woman who paid the price
When they met that boa

But man and woman soon stopped crying
And concentrated on multiplying
The woman eggs and the man supplying
The spermatozoa

Now endless numbers of their spawn
Are every instant being born
From Santa Fe to old Cape Horn
From Iceland to Samoa

And every single kind of life
Mates, breeds, becomes a man and wife
From sophisticates, sharp as a knife
Down to the protozoa

And every second every day
A blessed event is on its way
But O break out the beaujolais
This one is called Noah.

MUSIC

She got me early in my life
Cut out of me as with a knife
The part that lets you sing
O not the cords or strings or throat
She cut the inner secret note
The part that lets you bring

Sweet music pouring from the soul
With just a word my teacher stole
When I was only eight
My voice from me. She scowled and said:
"Wear shirt of white and tie of red
Don't come one minute late

And when we sing, you move your lips
But come Hell or Apocalypse
Don't let a sound come out
For you can't sing and that's for sure
God knows there isn't any cure
You monotone, you lout"

So I love music with a passion
But my voice is out of fashion
And I can hardly tell
If notes are going up or down.
I sing and see that teacher's frown
And hear her cursed spell.

MICHAEL

Exactly fifty years ago today
I put my suit on and adjourned my play
And walked five miles to the synagogue
With Mom and Dad through New York winter fog
And read the ancient words writ in the scroll
(No rabbi could from my throat song cajole)
I spoke the lines as if I understood
What each word meant, I did the best I could

Despite the fact that music was not mine
And on that moment I became a man
I found that words alone were still divine
And poetry became my master plan
If your path leads this way, give me a sign.
I'd like to help you anyway I can.

HART CRANE

Hart
My book is falling apart
That book of your great verse
Of poetry the blessed curse
Immortal art

Of every poem you wrote
And endlessly refined
And filtered note by note
Through the stanzas of the mind
The sponges of the heart and throat

Each page now stands alone
My lips rehearse the sound
I hear the great bridge groan
I see the sea where you are drowned
Each page a swallowed stone
This book's unstitched, unbound

Unreadable almost
The edges frayed to shreds.
Lines written by a ghost
That sing forever in assorted heads
In wooly noggins on a tropic coast
In fur-capped skulls of Eskimos on sleds.

DR. M

I know that there's a world out there
And for services rendered
Ethics, morality declare
That payment must be tendered

But when a tailor makes a suit
You take it home and wear it
If it's not perfect head to foot
There's no charge to repair it

And when the cobbler mends a boot
If your feet just can't bear it
He doesn't ask for extra loot
And that's the truth, I swear it

So, since I'm not a millionaire
Not even a pretender
Please let me know, is this bill fair
Or should I just surrender?

REPLY FROM THE DOCTOR'S OFFICE

Roses are red
Violets are blue
Send us that money
Or we're coming after you.

ON REREADING THE COLLECTED STORIES

I think of Spencer Holst
Whom we'd find standing at the door
All slumped and needing bolst-
Ering, he'd fall down on the floor
And then insist we take his pulse
Give him a glass of milk to stop the roar
Of ulcerated stomach lining tissue
Then he'd reveal the truly burning issue.

His latest tales about: The Giant Rat
That only Sherlock Holmes could find
The Language spoken by a Cat
Stories running through a Zebra Story Teller's mind
A Music Copyist or a Blond Bat
Ten New Knots, a girl who saved humankind
Tales of a black man out on the glacier
A raving drunk with a pocket full of treasure.

Story stuff out of fabric of gold cloth
Finely beaten and hammered and tuned
Clear and luminous as the Moon-Moth
As she floats on the face of the moon
Fit fare to be read while the sea froth
Marks the years on an island marooned
But to misquote the Mirror Story O so pure
Photography has no place whatsoever in literature.

JOE SCHEPPS

When Cosimo di Medici and Joseph Schepps
Along with other Renaissance men of repute
:n who have reached the heights and plumbed the very depths
Whose lightest words are law, whose judgements absolute
When they stroll out on Tuesday morn they let their steps
Their velvet sandaled steps tread a familiar route
These demi-gods, these jeweled ruffled charmers
Wend their way slowly to the market of the farmers

Across the golden cobbles of the castle keep
San Busco's mighty fortress greets astonished eyes
Its lofty spires lesser citadels out leap
And its innate magnificence electrifies
Straight thru the lawns and terraces our heroes sweep
While country folk step back amid admiring sighs
Displaying fruit, gourds and organic candies
For the pleasure of these lords and sultanic dandies

They circumambulate this early morning fair
Joined by some painters two musicians and a poet
And taste the cakes and pastries country folk prepare
hru out the long night's hours so that they now may show it
To lords and ladies who appreciate the rare
And who in fact would rather die than to forego it
They nibble, bite and munch on dainties thrust
Into their hands and mouths and chew with formal lust

While lutes are tuning up and painters making sketches
Our group of notables enjoys the changing color
An aisle of squash, a flaming row of ristras stretches
Around the stalls streaked gold by Autumn the Annuller
A nod and someone on the fringes runs and fetches
For Joe and Cosimo some coffee and a cruller
The poet pushes past a financier
And whispers these prophetic words into Joe's ear:

"Is not man strange? A thousand bucks a plate, Marquis
That's how successful fundraisers are always run
It gives the wolves a better chance of running free
Donations will not keep them from oblivion
So strange, despite my thousand bucks a word fixed fee
I left the price of my work up to you for fun
Advice seems to flow thru me like a sieve
If only I could follow the good advice I give."

A VISION TAKES OUR PORTRAIT AT WALTER'S

My
What an outspoken guy
Is there anything he won't say
Is there any subject too risqué
Or too sacred for the words
Rolled off his tongue like pearls, like turds
Whipped up into a pearl-turd stew
What are we going to do
With a fellow of this kind
Painting that stuff on our mind?

Out of the Kama-Sutra stept
A vision and our hearts all leapt
To see her skin so fair, so fresh
A vision in the living flesh.
Like old impressionists we sat
Beside the stream while we looked at
The camera and the vision took
Our portraits close beside the brook
And froze the moment there in space
Her dancing feet, her smiling face.
By candle light I try in rhyme
To freeze that moment here in Time.

And on the instant she appears
This fellow reved up all his gears
And with a flow so long, so deep
As if before he were asleep
Unleashed a primal courting song
Irreverent, lyrical and strong.
Just like the amorous sporting Zeus
When seeking mortals to seduce
Would change from his immortal form
Into a bull, a swan, a storm
Of golden rain — Now Jeffrey Lew
Was the vessel that Zeus spoke through
And holding forth he charmed us all
Beside the labyrinth where the waters fall.

A MESSAGE FROM UBU

UBU invites you all to dine
Help yourself to what's on the platters
Watch your wallets, the waiters are swine
Eat and drink up that's all that matters
This is a feast of words and of action
Understanding is the reward
A royal banquet of surreal abstraction
With a good debraining if you look bored.

So settle down into your seats
Here's a play that will damn well do ya
Tomorrow maybe we'll break out the eats
Keep an eye on the guy next to ya
No complaints if your coat is stolen
This from UBU THE KING OF POLAND.

KING UBU

Like UBU with his bulging strumpot busting
Out all over, like UBU always lusting
This play's amazing, brilliant, tastefully disgusting
Outrageous to a turn

'Cause UBU is the you you love to hate
The worst bad dream that you could orchestrate
To listen to him is to suffocate
To writhe, to sweat, to burn

For UBU has devised some magic way
To haunt our hours with his insane display
And on the edge of consciousness to stray
Until we long, we yearn

For freedom from his all consuming clutches
Ponderously lurching towards us as if on crutches
He reaches out, capers, his finger touches
Our minds, and now we learn

That we are intertwined throughout, much more
Than anyone of us had bargained for
UBU is us, our secret inner whore
To whose embraces we return.

THE DREAMSONGS OF HENRY NEMO

There is no consolation in the word
Nor in the touch
Is there milk and honey
No matter what you've heard
There is not much
That anyone can do or say
Tears cannot wash away
The wound a lover's left.

Only time, if you can wait
Can heal a bit the dreadful ache
The elemental rift
Only time can bring the body ease
And soothe the soul 'til it seize
The meaning in the drift.

———

God, send me down a knotted rope
That reaches from the sky
I must escape this envelope
So give me hope or give me dope
Or something new to try

Or send some agony that works
To clear my clotted brain
Devised by medieval Turks
Something beyond what merely irks
Some masterpiece of pain

To show me true oblivion
I hate the way time crawls
I cannot stand the way things run
I would, as soon as not, have done
Banging my head on walls.

———

A man must have a palace
A place to hang his phallus
To rest and drink and take his ease
To gorge 'til he convulses
To flutter female pulses
Partake of elegance and sleaze

A man must have his woman
To show that he is human
To fill his empty arm or lap
To gaze upon her beauty
To do by her his duty
To prove that he's the perfect sap.

———

Did anybody ever see
Such breasts riding so high and free
Like moons in lunar ecstasy.

———

He:
She's got an agenda
She's got a pudenda
If I were her Panda
I'd say with all candor
Let's go to the bamboo
I must dance the mambo
With you

She:
I see your advances
Your deep love for dances
But you're so old fashioned
A woman impassioned
Won't go to the bamboo
To just dance the mambo
With you

He:
We'll dance to the tango
Eat ices and mango
If I can't up end her
In my hacienda
We'll go to the bamboo
I must do the mambo
With you

She:
The dining and dancing
Sound very romancing
But will you take off your slacks
And dance the beast with two backs
If you do I will go
To the bamboo, you know
And dance there all night
With you.

———

Is it because I told you
That I love you
That your face is radiating
Like a star

———

All the joy I have in life
My lover scars with endless strife
She's found a wound and twists the knife

And if I ask why she does this
She'll list the ways I've been remiss
And leave me in paralysis

My stomach tied in knots of ice
My heart a bloody sacrifice
A million miles from paradise

My joy is gone, my love I'll hide
In that dark place deep down inside
Practice indifference to survive.

———

When the Queen of my Desire
Whom I would take to wife
Whispers those sweet words of fire
There's nothing more that I require
In this my little life

I thrill removing my attire
Prepare for playful strife
My only thought to satisfy her
I, the fool, the versifier
Wait, while she twists the knife.

HARRY'S ROADHOUSE

I recommend the pan-seared fish, of course
A grouper which just leaves me at a loss
For words, the way it blends into its sauce
So plump and succulent

Is every mouthful, every tender flake
There are no taste buds it cannot awake
No appetite so keen it can not slake
No tongue so impudent

It will not be completely overcome
No jaded diner's face so sad or glum
But will regain its equilibrium
Eating this sacrament.

GUY

A guy I've known for forty years
Or thereabouts, so it appears
Whose path and mine have crossed frontiers
Crisscrossed on land and sky

Our wanderings bring us close and then
Like all the wanderings of men
We part for years to meet again
To say hello, good-bye

In New York, Woodstock, Mandalay
Antarctica, The Milky Way
Miami and in Santa Fe
We meet and then we fly

And all the while that Trickster Time
Has fiddled with our pantomime
Making the casual more sublime
And I must testify

Like autumn leaves we're turning yellow
Age or wisdom makes us mellow
And my affection for this fellow
Grows, for this guy named Guy.

JOHNNY DOLPHIN

I asked a man to read a poem
He wrote a while back
We sat together in his home
As pleasant as a honey-comb
A cozy cul-de-sac

I liked the way the poem praised
Two women, what they wrought
The things of beauty they had raised
The flame within their souls that blazed
The battles they had fought

Against the beast who knows no peace
How they withstood the siege
Waged by the hand that won't release
Gestapo tyrant thought police.
So perfect, true and liege

Were they to what they knew was right
They stood alone uncloaked
In brilliancies of stars and light
That made new day out of old night.
I saw the man had choked

On his own words, a bit upset
Moved by the poem he wrote
Tears of astonishment, regret
I laughed, my eyes were also wet
A sob caught in my throat.

GOLDEN ANNIVERSARY

My mother told me clouds stood still.
I was a child in Brazil
We watched the world go by.
The thing that moved (the clouds did not,
She told me as we strolled the yacht)
Was just the deep blue sky.

The clouds were sets, the sky backdrop
That turned, just like a movie prop
On rollers, by command;
The world — a surprise Easter egg
With diamonds heaven could not beg
From Faberge's own hand.

She told me many other things
As winters passed and turned to springs
Always avoiding fact.
She concentrated on the mist
That, unlike reality exists
Before the actual act.

She drove her car with reckless speed
She taught me cards and how to read.
And Dad deserves applause
For being clear and practical,
Observing all the natural
And dietary laws.

Although in cars he grinds the gears,
It was from him I learned that tears
Flow when you're deeply moved.
Ancient tradition was his guide,
Accordingly, he laughed or sighed,
Approved or disapproved.

Now fifty years is quite enough
To drag your body through the rough
All by yourself alone,
But when you're so in line with life
To take a husband or a wife
Into the battle zone

And constantly come out on top —
I must salute you Mom and Pop
For racking up a score,
For learning how to penetrate
The mystery beyond the gate
Let's drink to fifty more!

ANDREW AND GAY

Now, Andrew, let me ask you why
Although the moon is full and high
It never falls out of the sky
But just hangs there glowing?

And why since paths crisscross and part
Meander, fade, return and start
Do voyagers despite a chart
Wander without knowing?

And when a journey, Gay, is done
Another one is soon begun
And on wherever rivers run
Wherever roads are flowing.

The way is dark and not precise
But worth the greatest sacrifice
A Pilgrimage to Paradise
Will keep your spirits growing.

Please get there, if you can, alive
But better yet try and contrive
To travel well rather than to arrive
What a way to be going!

A TOAST

Brent and Babz

I give you Brently and Babette
A finer couple never met
Both now and in the as of yet
They flourish intertwined
Like gorgeous trees they branch and leaf
And just their presence brings relief
No need to whisper, they're a little deef
Now that they've wined and dined.

I give you Bent and Babz and Co.
Including grandson, Dani, Bo
And may your numbers ever grow
'Til to the stars you're hurled
Singing a song that fills the throat
Tuned to the perfect inner note
That keeps this whole damn business afloat
Go fecundate the world.

I give you Brent and Barbara now
Come up and take a little bow
No, well we love you anyhow
Their modesty becomes' em
Let's lift our glasses high today
They're great, what else is there to say
And mighty flexible because if they
Don't know the tunes, they hums' em.

THANKSGIVING '95

I want to give thanks for the brand new laws
Concerning politics and other things
Especially the one exposing flaws
In ordinary men who would be kings
For now we'll see how fast a man withdraws
The hat he threw into the campaign ring
Now that the President's entire life will be
Broadcast on live twenty four hour a day TV.

There'll be a special channel to be sure
So citizens can tune in round the clock
Confirm with their own eyes the Prez is pure
The house and senate solid as a rock
This job's no longer for the insecure
Now that the law says they must all unfrock
Tune in, you'll spot the Prez right off, no one can fake it
Look, the senators are all half, but the President's totally nake

Here's thanks to laws that make available
All public buildings to the homeless ones
That make men equal and all bailable
Those who have money and those who have none
That let no man be unassailable
Because of ancient name or modern gun
That lets us choose what we eat, drink and smoke
And choose the time and place when we decide to croak.

126

And here's to that important social change
Made law, for which we all give heart felt thanks
Forbidding us from now on to arrange
Another meal from banquets down to franks
Without preparing on the kitchen range
Enough to feed one starved man from the ranks
For everyone of us who takes a seat
And feed them first! before we all sit down to eat.

Now Djordje and Betsy follow to the letter
All laws that are on books in our great land
And act as one, would rather wear the fetter
Than disobey the law's sacred command
And in this case they've done the law one better
I know that all of you will understand
If there's a little less for each of us to eat
ordje and Betsy gave the turkey to the village down the street.

PASSOVER '93

Come heap the table high with food
To stop our dining would be rude
Nothing should break our festive mood
I want your chair, let's switch.

Please pass that steaming perfumed dish
Of forest mushrooms stuffed with fish
To feast forever is my wish
This soup's supremely rich.

Wines from the valley of Bordeaux
Liqueurs green as pistachio
Beer, brandy, sparkling waters flow
All night without a hitch.

The sideboard groans with duck and lamb
Fresh shellfish, game birds, jellied ham
Hot puddings, pastries, candied yam
Our taste buds start to twitch.

One thing's for sure, the food's not bland
There's all you want served on demand
When dining with our friends Djordje and
Betsy Milicevic.

THE FAMILY MILICEVIC

The Bears are leaving us for Hollywood
Awakened from their hibernating sleep
They stare out at the winter neighborhood
A snowy wonderland some six feet deep
And for a moment wonder if they should
Back in their downy feather beds all creep
But then they hear the distant strains of triumph call
For them to hurry to that coastal banquet hall

Where one long dining orgy of the senses
From morning 'til it's morning once again
Takes place so folks can maximize expenses
While entertaining all their fellow men
Who having lost their natural defenses
Rate every single movie as a ten
As long as there's a bag of buttered popcorn near
And the degree of violence extreme, severe

But then, that's what the public wants, they say
They've asked for dribble coming out the ears
It makes me sad sometimes that this array
Of talent, Hollywood, these sonneteers
Who could be bringing us a better day
By blazing trails to ever new frontiers
Will settle for another Golden Globe award
To prove that they're still celebrated and we're bored

But I'm not here to Hollywood indict
But to Milicevics sing farewell
As they go marching out sometime tonight
To take by storm the Golden Citadel
I know they're going off to lead the fight
For Art and Truth against the infidel
To set the stamp of beauty back upon the screen
And put some life into the Hollywood machine

To stand up like a team of grizzly bears
Who never will give way to anyone
But face to face in narrow thoroughfares
Will make the other fellow turn and run
Back down a studio of billionaires
Who'll lose that fight before it's half begun
The family Milicevic with flashing claws
Never from Truth and Beauty's fight withdraws

So keep the fire burning underneath the pot
Of coffee or of sake or of anything that's hot
And work away most of the day whether you feel like it or no
And try to have a good time in between
For all of us are keeping an eye upon the West
And all of us are wishing all of you the best
And all of us know where to go when we all need a rest
And some of that Milicevic cuisine.

PHIL AND EMILY SCHEPPS

They say that the hanging gardens of Babylon
Were a wonder of the world and that Avalon
In floral elegance could match a grand salon
But here we have a spot

That's rooted firmly in a mountain place
Protected from the outside's madding pace
An island nestled in these hallowed halls' embrace
A magic garden plot

Like those where wandering scholars used to play
Their lutes and talk of music, art all day
So many hundred years ago away
That we almost forgot

The best traditions never are outworn
Small gardens mighty colleges adorn.
May student generations yet unborn
Scholars yet unbegot

Begin here at St. John's to earn their reps
And wear these garden stones down with a trillion steps
Let the first of them be made by Phil and Emily Schepps
And Joe, of course, how not.

LIVING TREASURES

Charles and Danny Bell

I think that life its own length measures
And there's great joy in giving
But as for me above all pleasures
Is not that you are living treasures
But that you guys are living.

THE CRYSTAL SKULL

Thirteen masters
For a generation each
Rubbed this crystal rock
To teach
The distance is
So very thin
Between the skull
And the living skin.

PASSOVER SERVICE

While traveling in foreign parts
Avoiding arrows dodging darts
And guided by some ancient charts
I bought from an Arab
I came across a manuscript
Half buried in a dusty crypt
Called exodus from old Egypt
Inscribed on a scarab

As I remember it the Jews
Built pyramids and sang the blues
So Pharaohs could forever snooze
Above the baking sand
Egyptian lords embalmed in spice
Lay in eternal Paradise
While Jews their lives a living sacrifice
Slaved in a foreign land

And one was born named tongue-tied Moses
One chosen by the God of the long noses
To free his people from the rubber hoses
The Pharaoh's men would wield.
By trick of fate he chanced to be
Raised in Egyptian luxury
Brought up within the Pharaoh's family
And one day God revealed…

But let's all drink a toast to Moses
To the God of the long noses

And one day God revealed his plan
To free His people from the Man
And thus to Moses he began:
"Early tomorrow morn
Rise up and go to Pharaoh's door
Take brother Aaron as your orator
Say let my people go we slave no more"
As deep as a French horn

God's mighty voice in anger boomed
God who appeared that day costumed
As bush that would not be consumed
Although it burned in flame
So Moses eighty years of age
Stepped up upon the Pharaoh's stage
To free his people from their prison cage
He called upon God's name

And gave his staff a little shake
And hurled it down as it would break
And lo it turned into a snake
Then Pharaoh gave a sign
And his magicians threw their rods
Which turned to snakes in writhing squads
But Moses' snake ate all the other bods
On each one did it dine

Let's drink to slavery's abolition
To Pharaoh's mummy's slow decomposition

But Pharaoh would not let them go
And thus the Lord spake unto Mo:
"Stretch out thine hand you and your bro
And wherever waters flow
They will be turned to blood" and lo
It came to pass exactly so
Before the peoples' eyes, before Pharaoh
And still his word was No

And so the Lord sent frogs, then lice
Then flies, then cattle paid the price
All of them dead to be precise
Then boils on everyone
Then hail, then locusts filled the air
But still the Pharaoh didn't care
He'd say "Go free" caught up in his despair
Then when a plague was done

He'd change his mind insist they stay
Then God sent darkness every day
So thick Egyptians felt it weigh
Upon their every breath
Until the Pharaoh cried: "Go free
But leave your herds right here with me"
"We need our herds" "Then stay in slavery
And it will be your death…"

Let's drink to innocent Egyptians
To God who caused Pharaoh conniptions

"If once again you see my face
On that day shall your death take place
You'll disappear without a trace"
And then the Lord dealt out
Of all His punishments the worst
The land of Egypt was accursed
It came to pass that night he killed the first
Born and a tremendous shout

A shout throughout the land a cry
Went up from every mouth unto the sky
Because in every house at least one did die
Except among the Jews
For God had given strict instruction
On how they could avoid destruction
And more important than mere reproduction
He said they must forever fuse

The image of this holy day
Upon their souls and never stray
In the least detail from this holy way
For God said: "Kill a lamb
And smear its blood upon the door
Tonight when I do what I swore
And smite Egyptian first born by the score
I God of Abraham…"

We must drink up for Abraham
To the blood of the sacrificial lamb
To the God of those who eat no ham

"I shall Passover the marks of red
While filling Egyptian homes with dead
This night eat ye unleavened bread
And ye must eat in haste
There is no time for dough to rise
Eat bitter herbs to symbolize
The pain of bondage and to memorize
Forever slavery's taste"

And Pharaoh called for Moses in the middle of the night
"Begone with all your people thou accursed Israelite"
And so six hundred thousand folk on foot began their flight
And then the manuscript
Went on: "And this day shall be unto you for a memorial"
Spake God unto His children God the incorporeal
"And ye shall keep it as a feast for time immemorial
How I brought you out of Egypt

And went before to lead the way
By night a flaming pillar, a ray
In a pillar of cloud I led by day
I led you in my glory
Remember how I divided the sea
Gave you water from stone, from the sky toast and tea
Gave you a commandment on adultery
But all that's another story"

Now eat we this unleavened bread
With bitter herbs as the Lord said
And drink to God the fountainhead

That's why we celebrate the miracle
Of Passover it's just empirical
And sometimes the Lord likes to hear it told lyrical

So remember
The Lord of Hosts lays down some heavy shit
And He insists that all ye mortals hearken unto it.

ANTICIPATION

Anticipation — savor well!
It gives you twice the thrill
Realization ever did
Or fulfillment ever will.

DIPSY DOODLE

You are so dipsy doodle
It really strains my noodle
To think that you can think the way you do
I'd need an electrician
Who's more of a magician
Just to rewire and unscramble you

Because your brain's so daffy
A kind of mental taffy
I think that there is nothing we can do
So I'm calling for the van
Just as quickly as I can
Because this is a case of missing screw

A screw is missing, yes sir
Heard it from my professor
And it's quite clear he has an overview
So we're sending you abroad
Medication, room and board
A good long rest's about the best that we can do.

POLITICS

To my lord the Mayor
And every other player
Of note and of renown
To all who call this town
Their home. Let's take a look
At things and throw the book
At him who overfills his cup
At her who covers up.

I speak in general principles only
As one who is not yet so sad and lonely
To pick at nits, rehash the past, find fault
Or worst of all to try and catapult
Myself into the public eye and ear
Enter politics, get rich and disappear.

No, like B.Traven, from heaven sent
Who understood the ways of Government
I, too, believe that anyone who seeks
Political office thoroughly reeks
From self-interest and is unfit
To rule, and should be thrown into the pit.

HAVING KIDS

Now having kids is not an easy thing
For Fathers, for their work is never done
A trillion swimmers manufacturing
Each day to make a winner out of one
To make a golden winner out of one

Then to deliver myriads or more
When your sweet mate lets you know she is ready
To bring them right up to that little door
And send them on their course while holding steady
Delivering while quivering rock steady

And then to wait a couple months or so
To find out if one of them has succeeded
And then another half a year to grow
Then twenty more to find if he/she is needed
To find out everyone is really needed.

SNIFFLE

Now suicide is frowned upon
I know and think it's right
But still, the thought of living death
A vegetable without a breath
Who cannot see the light
Who cannot mow your lawn

Speed is the thing when you depart
No time to watch the fauna
When life gives me the finger
I don't want to linger
Next time I sniffle I'm just gonna
Stab myself in the heart.

HOLLYWOOD

I'd rather write a novel
That's never understood
Than be a million dollar
Whore in Hollywood

I'd rather ride a comet
To the corners of the earth
And sell all of my stories
For a fraction of their worth

I'd rather write all day and night
Love songs nobody could
Ever think of singing
Than whore in Hollywood

I'd rather work on jingles
That pop into my head
And turn out buttered ditties
For my crust of bread

I'd rather do it my way
But things ain't been so good
So, if there's any work at all
Call, and I'm off to Hollywood.

NOTHING

It was said he would amount to nothing
Like nothing, less than nothing he would be
He could strive and strain and struggle
Buy and sell and smuggle
While others gave it all away for free

They said his life was doomed to total failure
Disaster from the moment of his birth
His folks though wise and famous
Produced an ignoramus
Whose miserable life would not be worth

The poor candle burnt up in the playing
Not worth the flesh and blood and bone
The buttons and the straps of leather
That held his wretched frame together
Not worth a pebble or a stone

They said he wouldn't last another year out
That he wasn't even putting up a fight
They couldn't resurrect him
They said let's disconnect him
They said, they said, and they were absolutely right.

THANKSGIVING '92

I don't go out much anymore
I stay at home and lock the door
Curled in a corner on the floor
Annoyed, alive, and pissed.
If someone asks me out to dine
To break his bread and drink his wine
I say to him: "That sounds just fine
Send me the menu and the guest list."

"I'll bring my family of four
Of friends and relatives a score
Some hangers-on and several more
We'll be a little late.
Don't start without us, how's December?
Above all, don't the bird dismember
Until we get there, and remember
We don't reciprocate."

ONLY A CIGARETTE

They'll do anything and everything
They'll advertise and lie
To stab you with those bayonets
To sell more of their cigarettes
And they don't even get you high

Just think of the hundreds of thousands
The hundreds of thousands who die
And there's no antidote
For that grip on the throat
And they don't even get you high.

They say there's nothing to worry about
No reason to get upset
Those stories you hear
Are inspired by fear
Of your friend, the cigarette.

I'm sure there's not one among you
Who doesn't recall with delight
The pleasures of smoking
Of coughing and choking
Deep into the middle of night

The thrill of anticipation
And then, when the meal is done
A cigarette, what could be grander?
Those stories are all propaganda
Cause smoking is just good clean fun

"Daddy, why do you smoke so much?
Somehow I don't think it's right
I still see the tip
It's stuck to your lip
From your last cigarette last night"

"Pass me a tissue, my daughter
I'm glad you pointed it out
Don't worry your head
Just climb into bed
No problem, my good little scout"

"Daddy, how come you are smoking
Those burnt little butts from the tray?
You don't look too good
So maybe you should
Tell me if you're feeling okay"

"Dear Daddy, what are you doing?
You're blowing your smoke in my face
That tubular stick
Is making me sick
And the smoke is all over the place"

"No Daddy, I don't want to try it
Please, Daddy, not now, not just yet
My throat is on fire
It's like a hot wire"
"Shh, it's only a cigarette."

NICE GUY

It's nice to be a nice guy
And that's the way I'm built
I choose the smaller slice of pie
I cry when milk is spilt

I let the other fellow
Get the best end of a deal
I try to stay as mellow
As the guy whose hands I feel

Making money in my pockets
While he talks ecology
Who's down on nuclear rockets
But he's not nailed to a tree

Like real Earth Firsters do it
With a twelve inch railroad spike
Driven in the body, through it
So couples on a hike

And even forest rangers
Who are also very nice
Shudder at the strangeness
Of such a sacrifice.

BEAUTY

All that beauty
Covered with a shadow
All that love
Fading with the sun
All my heart
Beating on the doorstep.

THE DEAD

Where do the dead go when they leave this place
Where everybody's having a good time?
Do they just float out there in outer space
After departing from this world sublime?
They must be bored, I'm sure, there's nothing much
To do, at least as far as I'm aware
Or ill, and that's why they don't stay in touch
Do you suppose it's just that they don't care?

At any rate, things now couldn't be grander
All of you folks are in for a surprise
I'm calling from the Library of Alexander
Where they stack the dead like books to vaporize
You won't believe what I have to show you, I guarantee
Wherever the dead go, it can't be soon enough for me.

THE FACE

How fast the face becomes a flash of flesh
It slides right off the bone like mother's stew
Before you blink it's lost its youthful hue
And then in just a decade more or less
Collapsed around the skull, a perfect mess
No one would ever recognize it's you
You tell the young there's nothing you can do
You're merely sloughing off your mortal dress

Preparing for the universal form
Of formlessness, spirit naked as flame
That burns on unconsumed, forever warm
A fire forever wild, forever tame
As soft as the clouds of a summer storm
That wash away all vestiges of shame.

POET AND PATRON OVERTURE

Now don't you need a Poet on the payroll
To flash poetic license if you're stopped
To Cyrano-like feed lines for a hay roll
Immortalize moments that can't be topped
Who always can be counted on to stay droll
And Villon-like laugh while his head is lopped
Unmistakably, nothing could be saner
Than to keep a poet ready on retainer

The Poet lends a certain dashing air
A kind of grace, a subtle elegance
The right embellishment for an affair
Of state, of business, or of romance
The presence of a Poet shows you care
Enough not to leave anything to chance
Not to keep a Poet! What could be inaner
When one has a psychic, guru, valet, stylist, trainer?

Who else will turn an ode right on the spot
To celebrate the closing of a deal
Compose a cancion red-pepper hot
To accompany the triumph that you feel
Write epics for your mistress, horse, your yacht
And every day fresh wonders will reveal
Only the Poet has the perfect knack
To strip the Emperor's new clothes right off his back

Revivify the royal cloth and show
As if by magic what we've always known
That nothing is but thinking makes it so
That neither Emperor nor his new gown
In their magnificence can match the glow
That radiates from skin stretched over bone
Less uneasy is the head that wears the crown
When it's protected by the Poet or the Clown

The Patron needs the Poet, there's no doubt
To swat the bee that's always in his bonnet
To turn confusing mists that swirl about
Into a clear and melismatic sonnet
Only the Poet, merry and devout
Finds the right path and instantly gets on it
But then the Poet needs the Patron too
To stay alive so he can write this poem to you.

MARRIAGE

Ah, marriage! That ambitiously elusive pact
That solemn and most final act
According to the way our parents thought
Who foolishly believed that there was naught
That could separate a married couple
So strong that bond, so permanent and supple.

Ah, married life! Where every day's a dream
That slips into the next without a seam
Each for the other sacrificing,
All consuming, all sufficing
Love-locked in deep embraces, kissing
The world not knowing what it's missing.

Ah married! At the end of a long day
Years hence, when both of you are old and gray
And summertime and wintertime are one
Long ceremonial procession in the sun
As vines, that as they climb together, lovingly contort
I see you two entwined forever in such mutual support.

ON THE ROAD

O it's so lonely on the road
My head is bent my body bowed
No one to share this heavy load
I'm in a zero expectation mode

I mount a horse and I get throwed
Got wild oats that I ain't sowed
I'm feelin' horny as a toad
I'm in a zero expectation mode.

MILLENNIUM

The end of this millennium was marked
Not able to eat, sleep, shit, smoke or fuck
As if somebody accidentally parked
His brand new fully loaded pick up truck
Upon my throat and belly and remarked
On noticing me underneath: Good luck!
So random, casual was the hit I took
A thrown coat, sliding down the wall, that missed the hook.

But now I'm slowly pulling out of it
Some of those holy pleasures have returned
Here I am out making a night of it
With friends whose friendship has most brightly burned
Telling the last one thousand years to shove it
Although I know there's something we have learned
That there's an immutable link, a bond
Connecting everything, before, right now, beyond.

And all of us from stardust were created
And everyone to stardust will return
Within a billion years our sun is fated
It's customary movements to adjourn
Leaving everything incinerated
The earth a final funerary urn
So that our dust and ashes may be spilled
In space, new galaxies and life forms to rebuild.

So, what's a thousand years or so 'tween friends
Each hundred years a century will come
Time's just a way to count, it never ends
Ten centuries make a millennium
How fast or slow it goes, that all depends
A nanosecond is too long for some
A million years flies by in just a blink
For distant stars burning on the galactic brink.

And cuddled cozy round this glowing fire
We celebrate the passing of the years
If they, about our little lives inquire
We'll say, they're sprinkled with some laughter and some tear
We're ready for whatever might transpire
Knowing the spirit always reappears
And even living flesh and blood and bone
One day upon the Master Potter's wheel
Into new golden vessels will be thrown.

WALTER CHAPPELL

I remember how funny Walter thought
It was when Severn died
And left his clothes to him, who would wear naught
Except a ring upon his juggernaut
He walked naked with pride

In the garden, the labyrinth he had made
The circles of the maze
Sang back to him throughout his promenade
A lilting, soft and dreamy serenade
Not many nowadays

Have hearts that harbored such a placid lake
Of generosity
Of words and song that could make all hearts break
And make the sleeping leap up wide awake
In luminosity

He saw right through the outer shell of things
Into the very core
The throbbing center where the deep well springs
Play their own music on the inner strings
In perpetual encore

In golden notes of dripping morning dew
His lithe form incarnate
Stripped clean of earthly pain and residue
I see him laughing in the tall bamboo
With children, friends and perfect mate.

EXCUSES

"I would have been here sooner but my car
Exploded when I put the thing in first
And when I realized how very far
I had to walk an overwhelming thirst
Forced me to run into the nearest bar
Where I imbibed until my bladder burst
And then I tried my best to call you on the phone
Which didn't work because there was no dial tone

I hailed a taxi cab to rush me here
I didn't want to make you have to wait
But something noxious in the atmosphere
Made my poor heart begin to palpitate
I thought I better have another beer..."
"Excuses, friend, I cannot tolerate
How many times must I tell you, it's just good sense
Self justification is worse than the offense."

THEM

Someone else is always having a better time
Someone else is flying off to a tropical clime
It's somebody else who's living the life sublime
It's always somebody else

The guy down the street has bought a luxury car
I go to the movies and he's already a star
He dines on the eggs of the sturgeon, sweet caviar
While mine are the eggs of the smelts

Others can run the gauntlet and come away free
Some can rise up from the worst sort of adversity
Go into battle and come out untouched, but not me
No, I come away with welts

Believe me, it's not that I really like to complain
I don't really look on everyone else with disdain
But why are they, all of them, sitting there sipping champagne
So stuffed they loosen their belts

And what do they know of the beauty of music and art
How can they be so aloof, remain so apart
Why do they look at me, through me, so that my heart
In the glare of their stare, melts?

GHOULS OF MERCY

The ghouls of mercy at the hospital
Devour the flesh to save your bloody life
Called from your chair there in the vestibule
They lead you to the laser or the knife
Or to the great machine, the monster eye
That sends a beam of radiation thru
Your every cell so it can crucify
That renegade and cancerous voodoo.

You lie down in position on the slab
The mask locked to your face to hold you tight
Technicians war against cancer the crab
That clawed and multiplying parasite.
Upon this field of honor, life and death
You thank the ghouls of mercy with each breath.

CORAL REEF

Despite swamp, sweat, secretions vile
There's something makes it all worthwhile
Despite scimitar sun
A miracle beyond belief
It's sailing for the coral reef
On a long day's run

Down two dozen feet — protrusions
Fairytale coral confusions
Rise from the ocean floor
Moving weightless with the motion
Of the undulating ocean
Green grottos we explore

In every hole, nook, cranny, space
Through fissure, hollow, rainbows race
Like darting color wheels
In every cave a grouper waits
While amberjacks move after mates
We're swimming past like seals

Each vision, color, texture, grain
Stags horn, elks horn, starburst, brain
Is mottled, speckled, wrought
Into fantastic lava flows
The living coral slowly grows
Architecture of thought

Between the patches of the reef
Marauders swarm in high relief
Dangerous doctors dire
They operate without a splash
It's vivisection when they flash
Teeth of surgical fire

And coming at us, looking wrong
A pearl-gray suit quite twelve feet long
A kind of dreadful tux
With belly white and formal tails
This socialite always prevails
A Hammerhead De Luxe!

He circles, spirals, flips a fin
Veers erratically moving in
Stops to adjust his tie
He seems so elegant and slim
A fellow gentleman — to him
We're sandwiches on rye

Perhaps it's not yet time for lunch
For joining with another bunch
Of diners on the go
The Hammerhead pays his respects
Although he never pays the checks
For dinner or the show

This calm, this crystal clear serene
Breathtaking underwater dream
Of sea anemones
Is so profound that we forgot
Our breath is held. Beneath the yacht
We're rising by degrees

To surface on the lesser world
Where banners wave and hair is curled
A world of "makin' bucks"
Where every day some rotten penny
Will ask you if "you're gettin' any"
Where life's a game of knucks

Those precious hours underneath
Will linger while you brush your teeth
Only your senses drown
To leave the chamber of the sea's
Like leaving distant galaxies —
A long ride back to town.

HERACLITUS

Heraclitus said you never
Can step twice in the same river
Not, give me a sufficient lever
And I will move the earth

Heraclitus cut to the crux
Not by saying, let there be lux
No, he said everything is flux
Within this wide world's girth

Heraclitus is the name
Of the ship whose mighty frame
Will soon the oceans' reefs reclaim
From the approaching dearth

Heraclitus is a model
Not of standard endless twaddle
With which we tend to mollycoddle
Our youth right from their birth

But a paradigm for learning
That everything is always turning
So hearts and minds all eager, burning
Can know the world's true worth.

SPEAK OUT

While faking a recovery
I made a great discovery
Which I'll pass on to you
While dying in intensive care
And trying to act debonair
A voice out of the blue

Revealed to me in one swift stroke
That no matter who it was who spoke
No one pays attention
And just because someone remains
Silent while you're taking pains
To casually mention

The benefits of nicotine
The life style of The Nazarine
The details of some dreadful scene
It doesn't for a second mean
He's listening to you
It doesn't even mean that he's
Being polite or trying to please
By waiting 'til you're through

No, the only reason you can speak
And friends don't interrupt and shriek
Or wander off to sup
Is that they either drift away
Or start preparing what they're going to say
As soon as you shut up

So while I lay there in my bed
Pretending that I wasn't dead
Still talking, though in grunts
It came to me without to do
Why wait 'til someone else is through
Let's all speak out at once.

BIKERS

A gang of bikers came to see
If they might spend a month with me
And drove their bikes right in
They parked them on my Persian rugs
And worked on them while taking drugs
Like speed and mescaline

I didn't have a moment's peace
The place was filled with pools of grease
My house became a shack
Where they would pace in leather suits
And hike all night in studded boots
Across the floor and back

The strangest things, I guarantee
Seem to keep happening to me
But this one was unique
I woke one morning after dawn
I stretched a little, gave a yawn
And went to take a leak

I opened up the bathroom door
And there was the girl that I adore
(I don't know what you'll think)
But she was pinned to the toilet seat
By two Hell's Angels, both in heat
So I turned and — I peed in the sink.

PERSONAL COLUMN

Self-poetrait

I put an ad in the personal column:
"Poet, cranky and demanding,
Seeks infinite understanding."

The letters started pouring in,
Inviting me to join in sin,
In sex by telephone,
Imploring me to be their mate,
To watch them while they masturbate.
One, from a girl named Joan

Insisted that I drop on by
And all her limbs quite tightly tie
And bind her up in chains.
She went so far as to suggest
That I wear nothing but a rubber vest.
Another one complains

That I don't love her anymore,
That life is such a dreadful bore
She's filling up the tub
To drown herself, unless I make amends
By taking her and some special friends
To a fancy uptown club.

"I am equipped to fill your needs"
Another correspondent pleads,
"If life has double-crossed ya
I'll show you how to find the way.
I can squeeze you in for a matinee,
But, buddy, it'll cost ya."

A postcard from a girl called Madge
Tells me that while the moon's in Sag
She can't concentrate on scything
Down on the farm — she's a pioneer
She says the strangest things, she writes: this year
I'll have Uranus writhing.

A Swedish girl, the name reveals,
Lindstrom, loves fast automobiles
Wants something just for laughs,
Sophisticated dinners, dance
Maybe a little subdued dominance.
She sent some photographs

Which still are hanging on my wall.
In fact, you know, I gave her a call,
She sounded just too good
Outside her door I smelled perfume
Before she let me in the room
She made me wear a hood

Which fastened tight around my throat.
She said that I would now devote
All my remaining days
To pleasing her, starting right now,
In every style and anyhow,
In all possible ways.

I thought this was a bit too thick,
Her coming on so strong, so quick.
I said I'd like a drink,
And how about the dinner, dance?
Instead she started taking off my pants
And led me to the sink.

She took the covering off my head
Only after we were in bed:
"Und now ve vill begin."
She had me start and stop and pause
By regulating tempo with her claws
Like baton strokes on my skin.

So there we were, completely nude,
Passing a pleasant interlude,
At least she seemed content.
But I was at a loss to see
That this was the way to understand me
It made me impotent,

Not that it mattered very much.
She didn't care to feel the touch
Of anything but tongue.
It made no difference, not a bit,
If a man's member was small as his tit
Or monumentally hung.

Somehow I got away from her
While she was modeling some fur
Full-cut Swedish sweaters
And so wrapped up in her charade
I left, and slammed the door like a grenade.
At home a pile of letters

Was waiting for me, bills, the rent,
A couple dozen dripping scent,
Ten with lipstick kisses,
A few were tied with ribbons, lace
Incredible, in every single case
They were all from lonely misses

Who were left there on the landing,
All seeking infinite understanding
Not prepared to give it.
Invitations to séances,
Cards demanding quick responses,
Letters that were livid

With despair and anger, sorrow,
Breakfast for first thing tomorrow
With overweight gourmets.
Lewd suggestions from non-smokers,
Subtle hints from marriage brokers,
Love notes from runaways.

I never called another one.
I removed my ad from The Daily Sun
And lost my appetite.
Some things, I guess, you just can't bear,
But I'll always remember the Swedish Affair
And the words she spoke that night:

"You're not too good," she said to me
While I was struggling to get free.
"Also you're not so young.
Take my advice, perfect your skills
By rolling giant stones up hills
While using yust your tongue."

It seemed a novel way to train
So classical, yet so insane,
I tried it on a trip.
But I wonder if this form of sport
Was responsible for the monstrous wart
That sprouted on my lip.

I never could make up my mind,
I'd race ahead then lag behind,
I just felt insecure.
People watching were derisive
Yes, in those days I used to be indecisive
But now — I'm not so sure!

THE DUMMY
Self-poetrait

Smoking this stuff all night and day
Affects the memory, they say
Even the chromosomes
Makes you stumble, falter, amble
Stammer, stutter, alter, ramble
So I just write the poems

And let the dummy say these things
While I sit back and pull the strings
And you guys watch the show
There's always someone in the crowd
Who speaks his inner thoughts out loud
Somebody says: "I know

He's real — just watch the way he moves
No dummy has so many grooves
Between such beady eyes!
It's just some wreck the poet found
Broken — he picked him off the ground
Just look how hard he tries

To pull it off — his stance, his clothes
That un-dummylike fleshy nose
Is giving him away!
A dummy has some kind of class
But this buffoon will never pass
I think he's going to say

Something in his defense to prove
He's a dummy. It would behoove
This chap to realize
That dummies are not made, but born
This creature looks like he was torn
Half out of his disguise!

How can he stand there unabashed
And pile before us mounds of mashed
Potatoes, with gravy?
Does he expect us to swallow
Everything he says — to follow
This broken and wavy

Extravaganza, diatribe?
Is it a speech? Come on let's bribe
Someone to let us out
This fellow's unprovoked harangue
Deserves an immediate meringue
To decorate his snout."

And then a pie somebody throws —
But wait, Rose', this story grows
Beyond the bounds, the bend
It must be stopped, or else like fruit
Too ripe, drop rotten at the root
Hold tight! This is THE END.

EPILOGUE

So, you'd like to have your poetrait sketched?
It's not unusual, far-fetched
To want your name in history etched
In myth and legend heard.
Don't think that just the rich and bored
Only an Emperor or Lord
Could ever possibly afford my fee.
Why, that's absurd!

This is the time to have it done
Save yourself from oblivion
Become immortal, number one
Break away from the herd.
Start the stampede in setting trends
Yes, take advantage now, my friends
Before this special offer ends —
Only a thousand bucks a word.

About Rosé

Rosé was born deep in the Bronx in 1934. He began crafting his poetry attending a number of colleges during the 50's. After a stint in the army he bounced around working as a lifeguard, masseur and astrology writer.

He saw his heaviest combat duty teaching High School English in New York. In the early sixties he assiduously pursued Ancient Greek while dining on Mexican beaches, toping in European cafés and slumming in Moroccan dives. Between a stint of acting, including the movie "The Edge," he published a book of drawings and launched skin diving trips throughout the Yucatan and the Florida Keys. His "School of the Night" specialized in occult classes and his "Liquid Wedge Gallery" made media history with sculptor Tony Price's first "Atomic Art Show" in NYC in 1969.

In 1980 Rosé started his epic poem "The Pearl Upon the Crown," still a grand work in progress. He performs as stand-up poet in salons, homes, theatres, clubs, sushi bars, on radio and television in New York, Los Angeles, Miami and Santa Fe. Rosé now lives in Santa Fe, New Mexico.

Other Poetry Books from Synergetic Press

OFF THE ROAD, Johnny Dolphin

This guy lives life, travels everywhere, does everything and transforms his adventures, his thoughts and dreams into living poetry. His confident voice strikes poems out of bedrock.

This Dolphin, master smith, Carves thru chaff to pith, Hammers
matter into myth.   *Rosé*
Paperback   158 pgs. $14.95

WILD, Johnny Dolphin

This collection of poetry, aphorisms, and short. Dolphin contemplates life, from the gutter to the galaxy, in a style best described as a synergy of Mayakovsky, Blake, Whitman, Joyce, Brecht, Burroughs, Khayyam and Baudelaire.

Johnny Dolphin conjures up a universe that is complete and
unexpectedly satisfying.   *Bruce Connolly, Library Journal*
Paperback   138 pgs $7.95

THE DREAM AND DRINK OF FREEDOM, Johnny Dolphin

This is a collection of poems written between 1946 and 1986, chronicling both a personal and a social history of the essence of America.

His dream and drink of freedom is the same original dream that
has produced the best inspiration of America.   *Paul Foreman*
Paperback   84 pgs. $5.95

ON FEET OF GOLD, Ira Cohen

This is a long awaited for selection of poetry reflecting Ira's many years of travel and living in the mystic lands of India and Nepal, the burning chaos of Beirut, the controlled city of Amsterdam, and the images of NY.

The scope and power of ON FEET OF GOLD puts Ira Cohen at the
forefront of American poets today.   *Uri Hertz, Poetry Flash*
Paperback   148 pgs. $7.95

POETRY LONDON/APPLE MAGAZINE VOL. 2, Edited by Tambimuttu

This volume, one of the last publications made by the magazine's founder and original editor Tambimuttu, is a collection of work from the new vanguard including Robin Williamson, William Burroughs, Lawrence Durrell, Iris Murdoch, Hugo Williams and many more.

It is only in Poetry London that I can consistently expect to find
new poets who matter.   *T.S. Elliot*
Paperback   96 pgs. $14.95

VISIT OUR WEBSITE FOR COMPLETE LIST AND ORDERING DETAILS.
www.synergeticpress.com